HOW TO SURVIVE RETIREMENT IN CANADA

(Self-Counsel Series)

by

Henry S. Hunnisett

INTERNATIONAL SELF-COUNSEL PRESS LTD.

Vancouver   Toronto

First Edition -- March 1975

ISBN 0 - 88908 - 017 - 8

Printed in Canada

Self-Counsel Series is published by:

INTERNATIONAL SELF-COUNSEL PRESS LTD.

Head & Editorial Office
306 West 25th Street
North Vancouver, B.C.
Phone (604) 987-2412

Toronto Sales Office
Phone (416) 691-8116

Eastern Warehouse
R.R. #1
Pefferlaw, Ontario
Phone (705) 437-2565

TABLE OF CONTENTS

FOREWORD -- THE NEED AND THE SOLUTIONS

FOREWORD

THE NEED AND THE SOLUTIONS

A substantial percentage of employees are now faced with forced retirement at, perhaps, sixty-five years of age, regardless of whether they are able or willing to carry on successfully with their jobs. It is a recent development and it is happening mainly to a group of persons who, until recent years, did not expect to retire until forced to do so by natural causes and at a much later age. As a result, they are not prepared for it.

It was thought that the retirement with a pension would be welcome, and would always assure a happy period of life. This is often not the case and many retired persons are disillusioned.

Fortunately, the basic causes of this unhappiness are easily recognized, and it is possible to assist in their correction.

Much of the writing on the subject is in general terms and is not sufficiently specific to be of definite assistance to the person who needs it. This book, therefore, aims to help anyone recognize the source of the problems which he or she has, and then to give a wide range of different suggestions to assist in their solution.

While the problems arise after retirement, they can be headed off by adequate preparation before the day arrives, and those who must cope with them after retirement can do so successfully. This book is, therefore, written not only to assist the persons preparing for retirement, but to help those who are already there with their adjustments.

As the great majority are married, this text is written to take into account not only the retired persons, but the impact that retirement will have on the partner and their joint relationship.

Although most employed persons retiring will be men, this book is written to be equally applicable to the retiring woman. The terms "husband" and "wife" are not usually used. The text is written for you, whoever you may be, and your married partner is referred to as your spouse. Both husband and wife should read this text, not only to help themselves, but to assist in understanding the partner's side of the change and to recognize when help is required and how it should be given.

Those of you who are single will find that the book also discusses your problems and offers reasonable solutions for them.

Everyone from early adulthood on should benefit and profit from the picture of the progression of life into later years that this book presents.

CHAPTER 1

RETIREMENT -- A PLACE IN THE SUN?

Retirement -- a picture of the "senior citizen," relaxing, soaking up the sun in contentment through those golden years. This is what the conventional wisdom would have us believe that retirement means. But is it really so? Certainly it is meant to be that way. But, if one talks to a broad sample of retired persons, a different picture emerges. Some, it is true, are very happy -- they have never enjoyed themselves as much before. But the majority are unhappy and wish they could return to work and the life they knew during their working years.

Obviously, something has gone wrong. It was always thought that, if people were released from their jobs at an age when still physically active and were provided with an income which enabled them to live in reasonable comfort, they would have an automatic passport to happiness. Obviously this has not been the usual experience. Why? There are enough people who are happy in retirement to make it possible to examine the situation, to consider why they are happy and, at the same time, compare them with the others in similar circumstances who are not. Such a comparison could yield the solution for those with problems.

It is only in the last few years that persons forced into retirement have emerged in sufficiently large numbers to make their reaction a visible problem of social significance. Much investigation is underway, and the predicted understanding is emerging. The result is that those in or facing retirement can learn about it through reading or personal counselling, and the great majority can hope to control those factors that are controllable. By overcoming their problems, they can assure themselves of a very satisfying and useful life.

To assist in **your** quest is the purpose of this book.

Retirement -- A New Life Cycle, It's Yours!

An automatic washing machine performs by going through a series of distinct cycles -- washing, rinsing and drying. When one has finished, the next, which does a different job, starts, runs until it has completed its function and then is followed by its successor. Similarly life, which begins with infancy, is followed by childhood to provide the opportunity of acquiring growth, education and experience in human relations. These are the necessary preparations for the next and longest cycle -- the working life, during which one devotes the best parts of one's days to employment in or outside the home.

This provides the income for each person's support and that of any dependants, raises the family and, what is now important, lays the base for retirement. You give the best part of your days and your strength to the task. It is an obligation which comes first, before any other desires. Then, on the day of retirement, this cycle grinds to a halt. It is finished, period.

If, up to this stage, you have been employed, it is understood that you are now released from the obligation of daily work and have the right henceforth to use each and every day as you wish. It is a new game with a new team, played on a new field. Points are scored for making entirely new goals from those which previously counted. The rules are new but simple -- you and your spouse enjoy yourselves!

Retirement Day -- What Changes Does It Bring?

On the day of retirement you terminate the life style which began the day you started school, usually about sixty years ago! During this long period, you progressed through childhood, adolescence, adulthood and perhaps you married, had children and raised them. They, in turn, reached maturity, struck out on their own and now have gone on to repeat the cycle. While your life was inexorably advancing through these phases, there was one factor which you could not shake and which was common to them all: the demand to conform to a schedule set up by others. It controlled your time. This is the big change in retirement -- respecting time. It is yours and uncontrolled and you must learn to plan for its use yourself.

Your first experience was going to school daily and observing the time schedule laid down. It grew more demanding with age and, when you became an adult and acquired the family responsibilities, these demands became more important. Your need to satisfy them lest you lose that all-important job which supported you and your family became more dominant. Always, this was the pillar of fire which you followed. All activities had to take these demands into account and your life was built around them.

Overnight, on retirement, all this ceases. On the first morning, there is silence. You have no demands upon your time. There is nowhere you must go, no one you must obey, no job you must do to earn your income. Is this not good? Well, there is a joker unless you have prepared for this day. Most people soon find that, not only is there nothing they **must** do, but there is little they can **find** to do. They are bored stiff and this is worse than working. The change has been too great, too sudden and they are not prepared for it.

Here is a typical example of what can happen. Charley "No Plan" had always said that he would never work past the age of sixty. He made some preparations for retirement. Successful financial planning assured him of an adequate income. At the age of fifty-five he had purchased a new home in a suitable location, and containing a well-lighted studio for painting, the activity he thought would be his major interest. He anticipated retirement with great enthusiasm. The day arrived with its final pay-off, separation certificate, handshakes, good wishes and remarks like, "You lucky dog, wish I was going with you." Charley went off home, but somehow things seemed different from what he had expected. When he could spend all the time he wished in his studio it didn't seem too attractive.

Time hung heavily on his hands. He got in his wife's way and she found his injection into her housework and daily routine annoying.

Finally, one day when guests were coming in the evening, Charley announced that he would polish the furniture.

His wife snapped back, "Why? Haven't I done it well enough to suit you?" This was not like her. He got the message and realized that his constant presence at home was bothering her. So he went back to the office where he had worked to see about a job. Fortunately, there was temporary work available on a project which was to be completed in a few months. This gave him the opportunity of getting back to the job again and, while there, to form a more realistic picture of what retirement life would be like, to make adequate plans and to prepare himself and his wife for it.

This gives the key: understand and prepare.

What are the problems and how do you handle them? If you have already retired, you will work on problems which exist. You have the benefit of the actual experience. However, if you are just coming to retirement, you must try and guess what will occur and what you will desire. The balance of this book will assist you in evaluating your life to date, in preparing for retirement, in coping with its problems and in enriching your life once it has arrived.

What Do You Prepare For?

There are three major areas in which retired persons have problems. The first is money. It is elementary that freedom from financial problems is essential to peace of mind and contentment. If income doesn't meet expenditures, is there much you can do? There certainly is, perhaps much more than you think! It is possible that the more intelligent use of the assets which you have may increase the income from them substantially and, if you are willing to make reasonable concessions and adjustments in your spending habits, you may well end up in a much better position than expected.

The second problem area is the use of time. It is real. The fact that your time has not been your own has meant that you may not have built up activities that can be continued as a source of pleasure in retirement. You have never learned to plan your time and use it according to your own desires. Now you must. But, once again, there are so many interesting and rewarding things to do that this should be a pleasure not a problem. There are organizations to help you find and

4

participate in these activities and very often major financial concessions to enable you to do so. No one need feel that there is nothing to do. We will look at many of the possibilities and how to find and participate in them.

The third area of concern is your mental or psychological reaction to retirement. Many look upon retirement as a signal that they are through, of no further use, and life no longer has any real value, meaning or interest. If this book does its work well, you will end up feeling that, not only are you still needed, but that retirement is a genuine reward. It is given to you for a life of effort, the pay-off for those years of work, of doing your part to bring your country through times like the Great Depression and World War II, from the gasoline to the atomic and then to the space age! It is given to you by a grateful nation which, as proof of its gratitude, provides pension assistance, free medical care and many other useful aids. Accept these benefits as a reward. Enjoy the years and there will be no reaction which might be caused by unhappiness or frustration. Most fears are much greater in imagination than in reality. Once faced and understood, they shrink in size and turn out to be much less formidable than expected. Similarly, the fears of retirement are in reality only paper tigers. Face them squarely and you will find that they lack substance and can be chased away. They will disappear and you will be able to go on to enjoy those goals which you feared might be unattainable.

CHAPTER 2

YOUR NEW LIFE -- IT'S YOURS!

The Release from Responsibility

When the door closes after you for the last time on the day of retirement, your previous life style will be left behind with the job. It will be filed away with the closed records of your past employment. You can't take it with you because that life was job-oriented and the job no longer exists for you. You are now on your own and must build a life completely new from that which you have been leading. Actually, the change began some time ago when your family, if any, finished school and became self-supporting. With the removal of the job goes the last link in that chain of responsibilities which bound you to your job-oriented life. It won't come back. Don't try to pretend that it will. Realize that you are now the architect with a free hand and have the glorious opportunity to build a completely new life, but one with a difference.

The difference now is in your position on the totem pole. During those early years of marriage and raising the family, you were the "Atlas" who held up their world, the low person on the totem pole. You helped raise the children. Your satisfactions came through theirs. The children have moved on to worlds of their own. Now that you no longer have to hold that job, your responsibility has been taken over by another. Those who were the thunderbirds on the top of the totem pole have flown away and you and your spouse have risen to sit together as Gemini, the twins, on its peak. Obviously your position has basically changed. With those responsibilities gone, your efforts can be directed towards the welfare and happiness of you and your partner. Your joint interests are now the primary ones for the first time. If you are still carrying some of the things which you had for that family, such as a large home, it is no longer necessary to do so. You are free to decide what you wish for this new stage of your life. A tremendous load has, also, just been lifted

7

from your shoulders -- the necessity of the daily stint to earn the whole or a part of the income. For the first time, your income is permanent and not dependent on keeping your job! Income from pensions, investments, savings and rents comes in without work or performance requirements. Think of what that means. No longer must you relate everything to your job, or wind the alarm clock! Spend your days as you wish, your cheques will continue to come. The work of the past has earned today's income. Now the days are yours.

Home For Lunch!

These changes bring another most important one which you may not have realized and which now will assume greater importance. It is that you are no longer away from home for your daily work. You will now likely be at home and free, or perhaps forced, depending on how you view it, to spend seven days a week with your spouse. No longer will your days be spent apart. Neither one is accustomed to this and you can easily get on eath other's nerves. Very serious problems may arise, but their solution lies in the new programme which you will develop for the use of time. However, it will require co-operation and understanding to make the adjustments. You should think about and prepare for the problem, for it is a problem and it frequently puts much strain on the relationship until it is resolved.

How Is Your Health?

Those having experience with retired persons say that one of the things which they fail to do most often is to have a thorough medical examination. When you were a child you probably ran through the whole series of children's diseases -- you know them well: measles, mumps, whooping cough, etc. Those days have gone but you have not been forgotten. There are many other diseases which can affect people of your age. Most are probably due to a general wearing-out or deterioration caused by those sixty-five years of use and misuse. You may experience some of them and perhaps have done so already. During middle age, good health may have made a regular examination unnecessary. Now it's different.

8

You will likely need a doctor. He can be a great help and comfort to you in these years. Don't forget your teeth, either, for dental and oral health are just as important.

You should find out if both of you have a clear bill of health, how far you can go in physical exertion and if there are any limiting problems. Each of these factors is important. Here you are dealing with certainties and you can't fool anyone but yourself. If you attempt to do so, **you** will be the one to suffer. The knowledge that everything is clear gives you a free mind to go ahead with any plans appropriate to your age. If you have definite and permanent restrictions, know the boundaries which they impose and accept them. Do not warp your outlook in useless wishing that they do not exist. Concentrate on activities within your capabilities.

If you have some condition which is restrictive but which can be corrected, thereby eliminating bars to a desired activity, would it not be wise to consider this step? The examination may also reveal something which is progressive but controllable and action taken now could perhaps prolong your years of good health -- there may be much to be gained and nothing to be lost by having that examination now. You can't lose with odds like that! If you have not had that medical, don't put it off.

Attitude

Now is the time to examine your attitude. Its importance in enabling you to enjoy retirement cannot be questioned. It is a determining factor in morale, and high morale is sought by every competitor, organization, business or team. It is recognized as an essential ingredient in becoming a winner in any field. It contributes heavily to satisfaction and happiness.

High morale is based on the confidence that you can, and will, succeed. Often attitudes are shaped by ill-informed remarks which are made by others and accepted without proper evaluation. Put away your preconceived ideas. If you start out with the attitude that you are not going to enjoy retirement, you probably won't give it a fair trial, just to prove you were right!

When thinking about retirement, remember all those difficult days which were a part of your job -- the steady routine and the relentless, demanding pressure which you could not avoid. How often you wished to leave it! You learned to accept these conditions through necessity and you became accustomed to the daily routine as a part of your life. Such a deep-seated habit is difficult to break and you feel lost without it. Even if you did not find your work so difficult, was it really so enjoyable and satisfying? And if it was, are you prepared to admit that you are so mentally barren that you can think of nothing better to do? Must you be permanently anchored in that rushing stream which brought this time-consuming work to you and carried off your days in its flow? If this is so, work was simply a narcotic to dull your senses. Surely you can do better now that you have a free choice. Is it not sensible to give retirement a fair trial and start off with the attitude that you **can**?

For years you have carried on using the special skills and knowledge built up in your job. Little new growth came after a time and the strain of your daily work left no energy for the development of other interests.

Now, freed from these bonds, retirement need not be the bleak mid-winter of bare branches and withered grass. It is springtime again and new growth along the interesting lines of your choice can begin. With the acceptance of this approach, it follows that you will make preparations with an attitude of happy anticipation, feeling that you are headed towards a most satisfying period in your life.

Acceptance Of Change

The next step in making satisfaction a reality is to accept the fact that there must be a great many changes in your life. One of the major problems is that the retired fight these and attempt to cling to the past. We all dislike change. It means the loss of the familiar with which we have learned to cope and its replacement by the unknown. We are afraid that this may bring unpleasant and insoluble problems. However, the changes that follow retirement are different in one very important respect from those which were forced upon

10

you by work or other obligations. You may now choose freely the ones which you will enjoy. This should not cause a problem, so the fear is false. You can look forward to breaking free from the demands imposed by your job, the care of your family, or the fulfillment of the obligation imposed on a young person on the way up. Instead of a negative attitude of fear towards change, you should look upon it as the means of release from the old bonds and the bearer of the opportunity to build a new life according to your chosen plan.

Now that you have an understanding of the very different factors under which retirement may be planned, you will be ready to start building that life. But, before beginning, let us review these factors.

1. Forget the old responsibilities of job, family and earning an income. They are completed, the book is closed. Concentrate on making the days happy and useful ones for you and your spouse.

2. Realize the changed position in which your retirement has placed your spouse. Both of your days are being changed. Prior to this, much of your life was spent apart and your work done in different fields, often without consulting each other. Now you spend much of your time together, in the home, and the old routine is changed by trying to help each other. It is a difficult change and much friction can result. It will require understanding and co-operation, but it can be planned successfully. It is most important because living with a happy spouse will make this time that you will spend together so much more enjoyable.

3. Understand any restrictions or demands placed upon you by your health. The maintenance of good health will be much more important than ever before and the advice and assistance of your doctor will be most desirable. If you haven't had that examination, have it now.

4. Develop a positive attitude that you are going to enjoy retirement.

5.   Welcome change -- it is the ingredient on which
     the whole success of retirement depends. Only
     through change can the old be replaced by the new.

    These are the standards (or perhaps it should be, the
standard) which you use -- for everything you choose should
aim to contribute to the welfare of husband and wife jointly.
If it does not, look for something which will. The other four
factors are simply aids to enable you to do this. Now pro-
ceed to work out your plans.

CHAPTER 3

HOW MUCH DO YOU HAVE TO SPEND NOW?

It is of the utmost importance that, on retirement, you know how much you have to spend and whether this will pay for the life you plan. You should also know the cost of each item for which you repeatedly make important expenditures so that, if you must choose between things, it is clear how much will be saved if something is dropped and what the price of the new choice will be. Only with this knowledge will you make the best use of your income. Then there may be many ways in which those assets that you now own, or the money that each would bring if sold, could be re-used or invested to substantially increase your income. This might be a very necessary step because to be in financial difficulties will prevent an enjoyable life. If you are getting by, the availability of extra money to spend as you wish will provide a feeling of security and make it possible to have some of those unexpected pleasures which give anyone a lift.

The next five chapters are composed to help you to arrange your finances before and during retirement and perhaps provide unexpected income. The first chapter (3) helps you determine how much you presently have to spend after taxation. Chapter 4 looks into how you spend this money and shows that some of what you consider spending may in fact, result in saving. Chapter 5 shows how to estimate your retirement income and includes details of the Old Age Security and Canada Pensions. Chapter 6 discusses how to get the most for your money and points out the new benefits which you will receive such as government payment of health insurance premium and extra income tax deductions. Chapter 7 then goes into ways that may make all your assets -- home, cottage, car, insurance, etc. -- work to produce income for you. Each of these five chapters is essential to help you get all the income to which you are entitled, and to spend it to the best advantage.

Because your sources of income will be entirely new, the amount perhaps greatly reduced and the ways in which you spend it very different, it is essential that you make the effort to know the facts accurately.

You will be able to decide which activities now give you little satisfaction considering their cost. Often it is possible to eliminate expense without sacrificing much pleasure and, by so doing, to make an important contribution towards bringing your income and expenditures into line. By simply thinking objectively about your expenditures, you may find better ways which will save money and which otherwise would not have come to light.

You may find it to be a very interesting study. The possession of the facts enables a couple to eliminate arguments about what they can afford. It is all there in black and white, which simplifies the decision-making. If you dislike this type of work or if you consider yourself incompetent to do it, get the assistance of an accountant. However, before approaching one, you will need to obtain the necessary information for his use. Reading the next section will show you what you require. Remember, too, that while you may be busy and short of time now, once retired you will have time to burn and will be seeking useful and profitable ways to employ it. Planning your finances is one of the best ways.

Your records need not itemize every small detail, but should clearly list all sources of income on a family basis. All expenditures may be grouped in broad classifications which clearly reveal any problems that exist and show what could be accomplished by revision. There still is the possible increase in income to be considered in Chapter 7 but, without this initial information, you would have no basis on which to start to build your plan.

Determine Your Spendable Income!

All you need to begin is paper, a pencil and, unless you are a good accountant, an eraser. Have some plain paper for doing your rough work and purchase some sheets ruled with horizontal lines and with vertical columns for dollars and cents on the right of the page. These are available at most stationery stores and enable you to keep your work in a manner which promotes accuracy and ease of addition. Mistakes are avoided and the whole thing becomes more pleasant. See the way it is set up in our example on page 18.

It will be best to calculate a full year's income and expenditures in order to catch all seasonal factors. If you use the last full year, you will also have income records from your employment (T4) slip and an income tax return to use as a check. From these you can take much of the information you desire, so use them as a starting point.

First, list all items of income. There are probably more items of income and, very certainly, more items of expenditures than you can just sit down and recall. In order to help you avoid missing some of these, solve the problems which will arise and guide you in decisions, the check lists, on page 16 have been given for you to follow. Decide on the appropriate figure for each item of income and list all of them clearly, one below the other. Write an identification accurately so there will be no doubt when referring back at a later date. State clearly the details such as "full salary without deductions." Later, it might not be obvious whether you have entered the net or gross figure. Avoid mistakes -- identify clearly at the time of entry.

You must choose the time period in which your accounts will be kept: will it be on a weekly, monthly, or annual basis? You will be influenced by the way things are organized in your life and, basically, by the way in which your income is received. You may have been keeping records already but, regardless of what you have done in the past and how your income is received, start **now** on a monthly account basis.

Once you have retired, many more things come in and go out in monthly units so it will be best to start calculating everything in terms of months. If you must, convert weekly figures to ones on a monthly basis. Remember that there are months of three different lengths in each year, but the average is approximately 4-1/3 weeks. So, to convert weekly figures to monthly figures, multiply by 4-1/3. Some things are paid or billed monthly and no further calculations are necessary. However, many are seasonable or erratic. In such cases, find the total for the year and divide by 12. It will be best to have two columns, both annual and monthly for simplicity and as a check.

Now let us start to make up the income side of the picture. Follow in this order.

Your Income Check List

Earned Income
Employment earnings (gross)
Part-time earnings
Income from business
Spouse's earnings

Investment Income
Bank interest
Bond interest
Stock dividends
Interest on money lent to others
Capital gains

Other Sources of Income
Rental income
Room rental or boarders
Car-pool income
Hobby items sold
Service pension
Investments or capital items sold and converted to income
Gambling gains (losses would go under expenses)
Unemployment insurance received
Other

You may not normally have income under many of these headings, but list every source you have had in the past year otherwise it will seem that you spent less money than you actually did giving a false impression of your annual living costs.

When you have completed the income side, then compare it with that shown on your income tax return. This will provide a check against any omission of income. There may be some items you did not include in your tax return such as your spouse's income -- so make adjustments if necessary. Here are some guides for calculating the entries.

The first item is wages. Calculate the gross amount for the year before deductions, and divide by 12 for the monthly figures. Some persons advise using net figures after deductions, but this can be confusing. After retirement, most of your income will be gross -- that is, you will receive the full amount without deductions being made at the source. You will then pay any taxes or premiums due directly. Start off on this basis now and you can follow it through into your retirement records. The first entry is the gross item from your T4 slip, if employed, divided by 12. If you are self-employed, use your gross earnings before deductions in place of wages.

The next will be income from a second job, if you have one, or from any part-time work which you do. Again, take an annual total and calculate the monthly average. As this must be kept on a household basis, record any earnings made by your spouse. This won't be repeated with every item as we go along but, wherever both partners have items of income or expense, list all of them. It is best to enter them separately and identify each properly so that future checking will be more accurately and easily done. Now list investment income, separating interest on loans, deposits, bonds and mortgages from common or preferred stock dividends. Why? Because you classify them differently and pay a lower rate of income tax on dividends from most Canadian corporations. And, for certain extractive firms in the mining and oil-producing industries, there are additional depletion allowances resulting in a lower rate of tax.

Now consider earnings on property you rent to others. These include income from any property you rent entirely to others or from short-term rentals of your home or cottage. In this latter case you may list the income here and any corresponding expenses when we come to them. This is obviously the easiest way if you rent your cottage for a short period and the whole transaction is simple. However, if you own investment property with several tenants and have a whole list of expenses, it would perhaps be best to make up a separate statement for the unit and show only net earnings here on the income side.

If you rent rooms in your home, take in boarders or if children pay something towards the home, enter this next.

Perhaps there are other miscellaneous items. You may have operated a car pool or made things as a hobby which you sold. Any such income should be shown.

Losses in gambling or on investments (if made up out of your current income) are best handled by including them in the expenditures. This will show where the money went and may assist in deciding if such risks should be taken.

If an investment matured or was sold or capital gains were made, any of the resulting money which was spent rather than saved or re-invested should be classed as income for the year and entered here.

The last item catches any remaining income such as baby bonus, service or other pensions and income from a trust. If there is any income which you have not included under one of the above headings, show it now.

Add up the total. Does it look right? Often it is easily seen that there is something amiss. If it appears to be incorrect, check the addition first, the accuracy of your entries next and then, if the desired change has not shown up, review each item carefully. Often a second, thoughtful look reveals that an item is obviously wrong. Finally, check against your income tax returns. When satisfied with the result, you have finished the income side. It should look something like our example.

Gross Income (to nearest dollar) for 1974

	Annual	Monthly
Employment earnings (gross) before deductions	$ 9,521.00	$793.41
Spouse's earnings	306.00	25.50
Bank interest	17.00	1.41
Investment income (debenture interest)	849.00	70.75
Income from car pool	306.00	25.50
Total	$10,999.00	$916.58

CHAPTER 4

HOW DO YOU SPEND YOUR INCOME?

Now the way in which you spend your income should be listed. Here is a check list of the main groups to help you keep track.

Expenses (while employed)

Payroll Deductions
Income taxes
Canada Pension
Unemployment insurance
Medical premiums
Pension plan
Union dues

Utilities
Power, water, telephone
TV rental or cable

Housing
Rent
Real estate taxes
Heat
Mortgage interest
Insurance
Repairs and replacements
Maintenance
Furnishings
Installment payments
Appliances

Personal
Food
Laundry and cleaning

Clothing
Vacation
Personal spending
Recreation
Reading material
Medical (paid directly not deducted from earnings)
Dental (paid directly not deducted from earnings)
Private pension
Life insurance premiums
Public transportation
Automobile costs
Gifts and donations
Savings

Start off with the payroll deductions. If you are employed, your T4 slip will show you how much tax was deducted
at the source and the other items taken from your pay for
unemployment insurance, medical plans, company pension,
etc. Your income tax returns will show any additional tax
paid or rebates coming to you. If there was a rebate, subtract it from the tax paid. If you had a number of employers
during the year, or if you are self-employed, perhaps your
income tax return is the best place to find these figures
and they are likely to be accurate. Record them for both
yourself and your spouse as the first group of expenses.

The second and often the largest single item is the cost
of your dwelling. This may be relatively simple to handle if
you rent a house or apartment, but may be much more complex if you own your home. If yours is rented, enter the
monthly rent, then any other expenses which are not included
in it such as power, water, telephone, TV rental or cable and
heat.

How to Calculate the Cost of Home Ownership

See list on page 19.

If you own your home, rent will not be an entry, but
the utilities and the following other expenses will be. The
first are the real estate taxes which are readily ascertained from your tax bill.

The next is the cost of a mortgage and mortgage payments are generally composed of two or more parts.

There are several types of mortgages, the two most common being the conventional and the amortized. You must first find out what type of mortgage you have and what the payments include. These are probably a combination of capital repayment and interest, perhaps taxes and insurance. You must be able to separate these because the capital repayment is saving, the other items are expenses. The conventional mortgage often consists of a quarterly interest payment calculated on the principal of the loan outstanding at the beginning of the period. To this is added a regular payment, the same size every time, off the principal. Therefore, each successive quarterly payment will be smaller because the last payment reduced the principal on which the next quarter's interest is calculated.

If the owner of your mortgage or mortgages has not already provided you with a table showing the quarterly payments broken down into principal and interest components, ask for this now. (See table on page 24 for examples.)

If the mortgage is an amortized one, the payments are divided between principal and interest in a different way. A complicated calculation is made once the original amount of the mortgage, the rate of interest and the final date of repayment has been set. This calculation determines what equal monthly payment of combined interest and principal will be needed for the life of the mortgage so that all the interest and the principal will have been paid off when the last payment is made many years hence. In such a mortgage, the early payments are almost entirely interest but there are small payments off the principal. The portion of each payment coming off the principal increases each time until the final ones are composed of very little interest and a very large portion of principal. Therefore, your expense portion will decrease and your saving item increase each year. Once again the mortgage owner should provide you with a breakdown. (See tables on page 24 for examples.)

If you have a mobile home, you may have the same type of loan used to finance an automobile. However, it doesn't matter what kind it is. The same division between interest and principal repayments should be known.

21

Under mortgage or loan interest, be sure to put the interest payments to be made in the year for which the account is being made up. Further down, under savings, enter that section of the mortgage or loan payments that is a repayment of the principal.

Next, consider the insurance on your house and perhaps personal property. While this is often referred to as "fire insurance," it frequently protects you against many other risks such as theft and water damage. Often "personal property" -- your clothes, jewellery, furniture, etc. -- are included. Read your policy and find out. If you can't understand the rather technical wording, ask your agent to explain it. Rather than attempt to separate the items into different expenses, put them down here as one lump sum. If you have a rented home or apartment and do not insure the property but have insurance on your furniture and personal property, include that here.

Often the policies are written for a three-year period, with a single premium payable when the policy is written and again when the policy is renewed three years hence. If yours is of this type, divide by three for your annual cost. However, if the amount of money involved is large enough, you may ask your agent to have it payable in three annual installments. This is a little more expensive but is calculated at a very reasonable rate of interest. It may not only pay you to use this method, but may make your handling of finances much more convenient by allowing you to make an equal payment every year rather than a large one every third year.

The expenses for which you are billed are easily ascertained, the estimates are the difficult ones. Soon after a house has been built, repairs are required and these increase over the years.

They range from the simple replacement of washers in leaky faucets to the much more expensive appliance, electrical or plumbing repairs. Then there is maintenance of the grounds, upkeep, painting and cleaning. On top of these come the things that may be quite expensive but which will come as surely as the familiar "death and taxes." Standard roofs have about a twenty-year life. Plumbing in older houses, particularly if it is galvanized piping, will have to be replaced. Furnaces and mechanical items will wear out.

22

How do you estimate these costs? It is possible to find out last year's figures, but they can be a guide only, not a final answer. They can be used in listing last year's expenses but, as you will need an accurate post-retirement cost estimate, now is the time to look into it more fully.

This will also assure you that the figures on which you base your retirement expenses are real. If you have been enjoying a very inexpensive period in repairs and replacements but are going to face a heavy accumulation of them in the near future, you should prepare for them. Expenses seem to pile up one on top of another, often after a period of relative freedom especially from unexpected ones. Household repairs and replacements can be very large and, unless such capital expenditures are no problem, you should anticipate and be ready for them. Otherwise a series coming unexpectedly might cause financial hardship over an extended period.

If you plan to continue living in your present house, look back over the past few years and see what you have been spending regularly. Then decide if this looks like a reasonable basis on which to project your spending for the next year. Take a good look at the possible major items. How about the roof, furnace, appliances, plumbing? If they are all approaching an age where replacement will probably be required soon, you had better work out perhaps a five-year plan to cover all replacements and estimate an average for each year. If a replacement must be made soon, you would be wise to anticipate and make it in the off-season when the lowest price should be available. Leaving it until forced to act under pressure usually results in the highest cost and, perhaps, damage which could have been avoided. With the estimates and your past experience, you will be able to come up with a reasonably accurate guess. It may be high one year and lower the next, but you will be prepared for the expenses as they come. They will average out over the period.

Next is heat. If you have an accurate record, well and good. If you do not, the oil or gas company will generally be glad to tell you your last year's total. You had better check also whether there is to be a new price (probably higher) for the coming season and find out what this is likely to be. Figure it out on a monthly forecast.

If you are in a condominium or a co-op apartment, rent a mobile home lot or have some arrangement different from those discussed above, get a figure which covers all the related costs, including such things as membership in the organization.

(a) Conventional Mortgages

Principal: $3,500
Interest rate: 6-3/4%
Quarterly payments: $100 principal repayment plus interest
Date of issue: April 1, 1965
Date of last payment: December 31, 1973

Date	Payment Number	Total Payment	Interest Portion ($)	Principal Repayment ($)	Balance
(1965)					
June 30	1	$159.06	59.06	100	3,400
September 30	2	157.38	57.38	100	3,300
December 30	3	155.69	55.69	100	3,200
...	...	...	...	...	...
...	...	...	...	...	...
...	...	...	...	...	...
(1973)					
March 30	32	106.75	6.75	100	300
June 30	33	105.06	5.06	100	200
September 30	34	103.38	3.38	100	100
December 30	35	101.69	1.69	100	0

Payments decrease each quarter as the interest portion payable on the outstanding balance declines.

(b) Fifteen-year Amortized Mortgage

Principal: $6,000
Interest rate: 7-1/4%
Monthly payments: $54.41 per month for 15 years

Date of issue: February 1, 1963
Date of last payment: February 1, 1978

Date	Payment Number	Payment ($)	Interest Portion ($)	Principal Portion ($)	Outstanding Balance ($)
Mar. 1/63	1	54.41	35.70	18.71	5,981.29
Apr. 1/63	2	54.41	35.60	18.81	5,962.48
May 1/63	3	54.41	35.50	18.91	5,943.57

These payments continue on the same monthly basis until:

Date	Payment Number	Payment ($)	Interest Portion ($)	Principal Portion ($)	Outstanding Balance ($)
Nov. 1/77	177	54.41	1.27	53.14	161.32
Dec. 1/77	178	54.41	0.96	53.45	107.87
Jan. 1/78	179	54.41	0.64	53.77	54.10
Feb. 1/78	180	54.41	0.31	54.10	0

The above tables illustrate how the savings portion of the monthly payment increases each year.

Next, let us consider your personal living expenses, beginning with food. You probably pay cash for this item and may not have kept a record. However, little thought on the matter often ties it down fairly well. Most families follow a certain shopping routine -- perhaps a major trip once a week. No doubt, with the great change in food prices of recent years, you have had to be careful and now have a good idea of what your bill usually comes to. You may buy some items such as milk and bread more frequently. However, start off with an educated guess and then keep track. Keep all sales slips for each week and retain them for the year. Soon you will not only have an accurate figure, but you may also learn some interesting things about controlling your food costs. Remember to add any meals usually purchased away from home to this total.

Estimating clothing expenses is more difficult as they do not follow a regular pattern. Major items are bought infrequently, certainly not annually. So, perhaps the best thing for you to do now is to try and decide what you and your spouse will need this year and estimate a cost. Keep a record and see if it works out. This will also help you calculate for future years.

Laundry and cleaning bills can be estimated here. Don't forget the seasonal bulges that occur when putting away winter and summer clothes.

Automobile costs require thought and accuracy. Perhaps you have a charge account which covers regular running expenses and repairs, tires, batteries, etc. If not, make a very honest estimate here. Adjust for rising prices if necessary. Now list installment payments if your car is financed. As with a mortgage, these payments will be a combination of principal repayments and interest.

Ask for a breakdown. Include the principal repayments as savings. Subtract the net saving item from the total cost. The annual decrease in value due to ageing will be taken care of by depreciation. Depreciation is the estimated decrease in the value of the car during a certain period, say one year, due to the fact that you have used up some of the car's available mileage and the model is now one year older. It is not a cash cost this year -- you paid it out when you bought the car. It simply means that, when sold or traded, the car will bring less than its original price. The difference is the depreciation and, when calculating an annual cost, this figure should be estimated and included. Accurate records over the years indicate that a car, on average, depreciates at the rate of 30% per year. That means 30% of its value at the beginning of the year is used up in the year, and this must be subtracted from the value to obtain a figure with which to start the following year. The next depreciation is taken from this reduced figure and, thus, the depreciation declines each year. However, repairs increase often almost as quickly as depreciation declines.

Now add in the licence and insurance costs and you have a total for the year.

However, if you have capital tied up in your car, that money could earn 8-1/2% interest or more in even bank and trust company investments, so you are foregoing at least $85 income for every $1,000 invested in your car. Keep that in mind for future reference, but do not enter it in this calculation.

Estimated Automobile Expenses

Consider a one-year-old car worth $3,000 at the beginning of the year.

Estimated mileage: 10,000 miles of combined
    city and country driving
Depreciation calculated at 30% of value at beginning of year

	$ 900
Licence	45
Insurance	175
Gasoline, oil, lubrication, etc.	515
Repairs, replacement	174
	$1,809

The above is simply an example. Replace these figures with your own. To these must be added any additional expenses applicable in your case, such as interest charges if the car is financed, garage rent and washes.

The Final List

The following example is presented not as an average family expenditure or one to which you should attempt to adjust your own. It is simply a listing of how one couple might have used their means and is for the purposes of illustration only.

How the Money was Spent in 1973 (to the nearest dollar)

	Per Year	Per Month
Deductions and Taxes		
Income taxes deducted at source	$ 1,564	$130
Other payroll deductions	355	30
Income taxes paid direct	29	2
Utilities		
Power, water, TV rental	251	21
Telephone	119	10
If Renting		
Rent	...	...
If Home Owned		
Real estate taxes	645	54
Heat	275	23
Mortgage interest	17	1
Insurance	54	4
Repairs and maintenance	310	26
Furnishings	400	33
Appliances	114	9
Personal		
Food	1,456	121
Laundry and cleaning	78	6
Personal miscellaneous	275	23
Clothing	585	50
Vacations	547	45
Recreation	253	21
Reading	85	7
Personal care	250	21
Medical and dental paid direct	295	25
Life insurance premiums	162	14
Public transportation	78	7
Automobile (see table, page 27)	1,809	151
Gifts and donations	242	20
Savings	751	63
	$10,999	$917

CHAPTER 5

ESTIMATING RETIREMENT INCOME

Now that you have completed a list of last year's earnings and expenditures, you are ready to prepare an estimate of your post-retirement situation. By doing this you will know the truth about your financial position and will know what changes, if any, will be necessary. Use the same form as previously, but now you will have to replace your salary with new sources of income.

The Importance of Your Sixty-fifth Birthday

This birthday is often unwelcome and sometimes dreaded. But that's all wrong! It is an occasion for enthusiasm. Look what happens. On the eve of your sixty-fifth, the curtain is drawn across the stage on which your working life was played out. The next morning brings your second most important birthday -- the first of course, being that day on which you arrived. Then, Dad passed out cigars, everyone was happy, and you embarked on that sixty-five-year trip through the maze of events that is your life to date. Now, during this night, the scenery on the stage will be shifted and you will begin a new life. That calls for a real celebration! Invite your friends, family and also your local Member of Parliament, for it is he and his predecessors who have made possible this retirement at sixty-five with pensions. Invite Pierre Trudeau, too, even if you don't normally support him, for it's you and others like you that he had in mind when his government raised and indexed the pension and added other goodies for the retired. Don't ask Margaret, Justin, and Sascha for they would steal the show, and we don't want that. This is **your** day.

How often have you looked at those contests with prizes such as $100 a month for life, a trip to Europe, or some such

29

things and thought, "Oh, boy! What I would give to win that!"
Now, on this date, you surpass all those winners. Look at
what the dawn has brought for you today:

1. The Old Age Security Pension of $120 or more per
    month for life, and the same for your spouse when
    sixty-five, provided each meets the residence re-
    quirements plus a further "Guaranteed Income
    Supplement" if required (up to $84.21 if single
    and $74.79 each if both spouses qualify);

2. Canada Pension (if you are eligible) up to a maxi-
    mum of $122.48 per month for those retiring
    January 1, 1975, and increasing steadily with in-
    flation;

3. Possible elimination of any premiums which you
    have been paying for your provincial health and
    hospital plan (vary in each province);

4. Additional income tax exemption (now $1,174 and
    may increase) as a basic deduction for all tax-
    payers sixty-five or over;

5. Allowance to pool exemptions for pensioner
    couples if one spouse does not have sufficient in-
    come to take full advantage of exemptions;

6. In 1975 (and hopefully continuing after that) the
    first $1,000 of **private** pension income tax free
    (Old Age Security and Canada Pensions do not
    qualify);

7. Many municipal or provincial income or property
    tax exemptions and other benefits which should
    be enquired about locally;

8. Reductions on many public transportation systems
    -- in Vancouver, free rides; in Toronto half-
    price -- discounts on airlines and railways;

9. Price reductions for tickets for many theatres
    and other entertainments, most of which, with
    perhaps the exception of some local schemes,
    applying even if you continue working.

If that list is not impressive enough, you had better work on your Member of Parliament. But, for most of us, it will bring smiles. So draw back the curtain and start the celebrations. Paper hats, noisemakers, songs and drinks of your choice and perhaps some humorous remarks by Pierre. It's a fine way to start off on the rest of your life. And keep the party going as late as you wish, you don't have to get up tomorrow. The celebration is to mark that very important day, for those pensions and other benefits cannot begin until it has arrived.

Note: You must have a Social Insurance number to receive any government pensions or other forms of assistance. If you do not have one, apply at once. Forms are available at banks, post offices, etc.

Sources of Income

Check List of Possible Sources of Post-Retirement Income

1. **Pensions**
   (a) Old Age Security Pension
   (b) Canada Pension
   (c) Private or industrial pension
   (d) Service pension

2. **Investment Income**
   (a) Bank interest
   (b) Bonds and other interest
   (c) Dividends from Canadian stocks
   (d) Net income from investment property
   (e) Room rentals or boarders
   (f) Other

3. **Earned Income**
   (a) Hobby income
   (b) Part-time work

The Old Age Security Pension

This pension is paid as a matter of right to all eligible persons. Both husband and wife may receive it. There are only two qualifications -- age and residence. The recipient must have attained the sixty-fifth birthday and be able to prove it. A birth or baptismal certificate is requested, but if such is not available, there are other acceptable forms of proof. If you do not have either certificate, visit your local office of the Department of National Health and Welfare and discuss your case with them. They will tell you of other acceptable evidence.

Residence Requirements

These are met if you:

1. Have resided in Canada after reaching the age of eighteen for periods which total at least forty years.

2. Have resided or been in Canada for ten consecutive years immediately before approval of the application.

3. Have been present in Canada after reaching the age of eighteen and prior to the ten years mentioned above, for periods which equal, when totalled, at least three times the length of absence during the ten-year period and have resided in Canada for at least one year immediately preceding the approval of your application.

There are exceptions related to foreign employment by the Canadian Government, a Canadian business or international agency, overseas postings in the Armed Services, and missionary work. Enquire if you are in this group.

Application forms are available at post offices and should be submitted six months in advance of your sixty-fifth birthday so that your pension will start in the month following that event.

Payment of Pension Outside Canada

Once approved, pension payments may be made to you outside Canada indefinitely if you have resided in Canada for twenty-five years after your twenty-first birthday. If you are not so qualified, they will be paid outside Canada for six months only.

The Pension

Payment can begin in the month after your sixty-fifth birthday. If you are late in applying, it can be paid for one year retroactively. The monthly payment is now subject to change and is adjusted with the cost of living quarterly. In the first quarter of 1975, it will be $120.01 per month. There is an additional amount called the "Guaranteed Income Supplement" (a monthly maximum of $84.21 for a single, and $74.79 each for married couples if both receive the Old Age Security Pension) payable to pensioners who have no other, or very little other, income. Check the current figure for the pension when completing your income estimate.

The Canada Assistance Plan

If you do not qualify for benefits under the Canada Pension plan and are in need, or if the benefits you receive under the Canada Pension plan, Old Age Security Pension and Guaranteed Income Supplement programme are insufficient to meet your needs, you should write to your provincial welfare department in the capital city of your province for information about the additional assistance that may be made available to you.

Canada Pension

This is entirely separate, and in addition to, the Old Age Security Pension. They have nothing to do with each other and, if you are eligible, you **and** your spouse can have both. Eligibility rules are as follows.

1.   You must be at least sixty-five years of age. With the changes introduced in the autumn of 1974, it is no longer necessary to retire to receive the pension nor is the pension reduced if you earn money from employment.

2.   You must have worked in "pensionable employment" as defined by the Canada Pension plan and have paid premiums into the fund at some time, but not necessarily all the time, since January 1, 1966. Your earnings in any year must have been sufficient to have qualified you to make premium payments under the plan.

3.   You must have a Social Insurance number.

The monthly pension cheque to which you are entitled will be based on a number of items, the first being your pensionable earnings. This will be the total amount of pensionable earnings on which you have paid premiums since the inception of the plan in 1966. (Note it is the **amount**, not the premiums, which is used in the calculation.) The original plan required that earnings exceeded $600 if the person was employed and $800 if self-employed. These minimums have been increased from time to time and now stand at $700 for the employed and $900 for the self-employed. Premiums were paid originally according to a schedule of earnings up to $5,000. Any excess earnings over the maximum allowable in any year were not included. In subsequent years, this figure was increased to $5,600 in 1973, $6,600, in 1974 and will be $7,400 in 1975. Every time this figure is increased, it has the effect of increasing your potential pension because each previous year's total is re-calculated for you. Thus, the final effect will be as if you contributed on a larger amount in each previous year and your pension will be raised accordingly. The maximum pension will be possible for those retiring on December 31, 1974 or thereafter. Roughly, it will be calculated so that your final annual pension will be 25% of your adjusted averaged annual pensionable earnings from January 1, 1966 to the month before your pension begins.

Those retiring in January 1, 1974 who have earned the maximum since January, 1966, will receive a pension of

$98.33 per month. However, with the effect of the above-mentioned increases, together with the maximum 1974 contributions, the starting pension on January 1, 1975 will be increased to $122.48.

Once the pension is drawn for the first time, it is then increased annually with the cost of living, as follows. The twelve-month average of the cost of living from November to October is calculated and compared with the same average figure from the previous year. If this figure has increased, your pension will rise by the same percentage and you will receive the increased cheque in the following January.

One each year, before you begin drawing your pension, you are entitled to ask the local office of the Canada Pension plan to calculate the pension to which you will be entitled based on your pensionable earnings to date. If you do not know, enquire so that you will have a starting figure to use in calculating retirement income. The first step is to obtain a card from your local Canada Pension plan office, complete and return it to Ottawa. It will be returned to you showing your pensionable earnings to date and the local office will calculate what pension it will bring.

Note: The Canada Pension plan was amended in the autumn of 1974 and these now make many persons eligible for pension who were previously disqualified. Some of the changes are as follows.

1.   One can continue to work after sixty-five and receive the pension.

2.   There is no reduction in pension regardless of how much is earned in employment.

3.   A husband whose wife dies can apply for benefits if his wife was entitled to a pension.

4.   If a mother who was receiving a Canada Pension dies, her children may be entitled to benefits.

There are other additional but complicated changes. If you have been disqualified under the old plan, enquire to see if the changes affect your position.

Personal or Industrial Pension Plans

You may have either a personal or an industrial pension plan or both. Find out well before retirement exactly what your plan offers you. Some have options and you must make a choice. Do not do this without knowing, studying and understanding the long-term effects your decision will have. Above all, do not make a quick judgment on the sole advice of an insurance agent.

In the case of an industrial plan which comes with your job, you should ask through appropriate channels just what this pension offers. Don't be satisfied with partial verbal information. Get the facts in writing. Take them away, study them and discuss them with your spouse, accountant, lawyer and/or bank manager.

If it is a personal pension, purchased from an insurance company, you will have a formal contract which was given to you when you purchased it. Study this and ask advice as suggested above. Check with the insurance company to see if there are any improvements to be offered. Consider any alternatives from which you must choose on retirement. Above all, don't make a final decision respecting the kind of annuity you wish without studying your whole retirement plan and taking your spouse's situation into account should she or he outlive you. This is discussed more fully in Chapter 13.

Investment and Other Means

Income from previously-owned investments, room rentals, etc. will continue on and are not directly affected by retirement. They can be carried into your retirement income estimate unchanged.

Some income, such as that from your car pool, will cease, however, with employment and will be dropped.

New Sources of Income

If you anticipate new sources of income after retirement, include them but be careful. Jobs for retired persons are very scarce, have little security and usually offer less pay than they would for full-time younger people. Don't count on this source unless you have a definite job lined up.

Hobby income is also a very speculative thing. If you are now earning income from this source and can reasonably expect it to continue or increase, well and good. If it's only a hope, by all means work towards its development, but don't count on it to buy the groceries.

Preliminary Estimate of Retirement Income

The figures given here for Canada Pension Plan are based on retirement January 1, 1975. The figures for Old Age Security Pension are estimated for the same person whose working income is shown in Chapter 4. During the husband's last year of employment (1973) the couple's combined earnings were $10,999. After retirement their estimated income is as follows:

	Annual	Monthly
Old Age Security Pension	1440.72	120.06
Old Age Security Pension (Spouse)	1440.72	120.06
Canada Pension	1469.88	122.48
Investment income	850.00	70.83
Spouse's earnings	300.00	25.00
Gross income	5501.32	458.43

These figures assume that the spouse is now sixty-five years of age and draws the Old Age Security Pension. In most cases this will not be true and some provision must be made until the pension begins. As a retiring employee, you will be entitled to holiday pay and, perhaps, other items such as the three weeks' unemployment insurance which automatically becomes available under present regulations. However, you must apply for it. If these items do not fill the gap, you should prepare for it by saving, perhaps in a registered retirement savings plan. In any case, you should understand and know what to expect.

CHAPTER 6

YOUR COST OF LIVING IN RETIREMENT

Your cost-of-living figures are going to be somewhat different from your list of expenditures while employed. The first major change will be in taxes. You will receive your pension cheques and your investment income in full without income tax deduction.

If 75% or more of your income has been from employment, income tax has been deducted at the source and any balance due has been paid when the annual return was filed. However now, if over 25% of your income comes from sources at which deductions have not been made, and it probably will after retirement, you are required to make quarterly installments if you are liable for over $400 in tax (1974).

It is not our wish to advise technically on income tax, but you should be aware of this liability. Discuss it with your advisor. If you do not have such a connection, contact the members of your local tax office. Do not hesitate to do so. They are most helpful and you have nothing to fear in contacting them as they will give all information freely without asking your name. They are courteous and try to assist as much as possible.

A New Deduction

Remember, if you have reached sixty-five you are entitled to an extra $1,174 exemption in taxable income (1974). This is the first saving we record which helps reduce expenses for the senior citizen. Your spouse is entitled to the same if she or he has sufficient income to require it. If not, the balance can be used by the other partner.

There will no longer be deductions for Canada or company pension plans, unemployment, hospital or medical insurance, unless you start working again. In this case there may be deductions and you should check all public or private plans which have been paid through payroll deductions to ascertain if they now require direct payment by either you or your spouse. The private plans, such as Blue Cross -- Extended Care and many other health plans will probably require continued premiums to keep them in force, so do not ignore them, less they be inadvertently cancelled for nonpayment. This could readily happen if payment has been made through a payroll or another group in which you no longer participate. It is up to you to see that you go on a direct-pay basis if required. So check with your employer on retirement to find out if these are payments you must now take over personally. In any event, the sum total is almost sure to mean a very substantial saving in income taxes and other deductions.

If you do have a part-time job and taxes, etc. have been deducted, the full pay for this should be recorded in your income and all deductions recorded in your expense schedule. Even if some deductions are made at the source, unless they are taken from at least three quarters of your income, you may be responsible for making quarterly installments on the balance. Usually this happens if your total estimated federal income tax exceeds $400 (as of 1974).

Your Home

The next cost-of-living to be considered is your dwelling. If you continue to live in the same home, you can simply use the expense calculations made in your first schedule with any estimate for expected changes. If you decide to move later, you can make the change in a final calculation. Some municipalities have special arrangements for retired homeowners. Check to see if yours does. In making your forecast of retirement plans, you should realize that advancing years may make some difference in your estimate. Will you be able to continue to do some of the heavier chores? If not, include a cost to have someone do them for you.

Food

You may be surprised to find there can also be some reduction in food cost. Firstly, you may have purchased meals at work or, if you took a lunch, bought expensive packaged items that could be carried easily. Lunch at home now may be less expensive. Secondly, most persons find that they are not as active and eat less when retired. Usually, there is more time available for shopping and this will enable you or your spouse to search out special values and take the time to get the most for your money. It can make a noticeable difference and the time spent may enable you to purchase as much nutrition and have as much pleasure in eating on a reduced budget. Perhaps you can foresee such savings when entering your estimate of food costs.

Clothing

Clothing costs also may be reduced. Did your work require a standard of dress which you need not maintain during retirement? Frequently retired women devote more time to making clothing and this can result in considerable savings. Once again, what change will come here will depend on your personal circumstances, so make the best estimate you can. Laundry and cleaning costs may also vary for the same reasons as clothing.

Entertainment

You may wish to spend more time with hobbies and enjoy additional entertainment, because you have more time available. But, this need not mean more cost as there are two offsetting savings possible. The first is that you no longer need to go to shows, etc. at the expensive times like Friday and Saturday nights. You can go on "off" nights and to matinees. Rather than going out for dinner, you and your friends might enjoy a leisurely lunch. This is almost always less expensive than a dinner and may be less crowded and just as enjoyable. Now that you have more time, you may do more entertaining at home as well. The second saving will be

41

in lower prices so often given to senior citizens. Enquire from others who will know where these exist and how you can be sure you get all that is coming to you. You should also find out about special group rates and you will be well advised to start right off at the beginning to take advantage of them.

Transportation

Transportation will be different as there will no longer be that regular trip to and from work. Also, many carriers give senior citizens a reduction -- on the Toronto Transit Commission, you ride for half fare and in some cities, such as Vancouver, free!

Vacations and Travel

There are three basic savings now available to you in the travel area. Firstly, select off-peak season dates which are usually substantially cheaper. Secondly, notice that certain days of departure and return are often much less expensive on airlines, etc. Thirdly, consider vacation periods, which are often not possible for the working person and which may be more reasonably priced. For example, a 21-to-45-day transatlantic air fare is much less expensive than the 14-day rate. Resorts may give a discount if it is requested. Enquire and be sure to locate these savings rather than pay full price when it is not necessary.

Eliminate Installment Payments

Installment payments generally indicate the purchasing of larger, more expensive items of furniture, clothing or perhaps an automobile, at times when this cannot be delayed. At this stage in your life, it may be that you will have the option of delaying such purchases. In addition, while installment purchases are often desirable, or necessary, they include an interest charge at a very high rate. Perhaps now the interest saving makes it preferable for you to save up for a purchase and use the interest for your own benefit. If you wish to purchase on credit, borrow on the best security you have, to obtain the lowest rate. (See Chapter 7.)

Medical and Dental

Often the basic health plan will be paid for you once you are eligible for Old Age Security Pension, but there are usually some unavoidable expenses which are not covered by any insurance and which you must pay. You may elect to purchase a private plan which will provide extra protection. Enter an estimate for these and all known medical expenses plus a fair estimate for others which will probably come. Overall, there should be a reduction of substantial proportions in this category.

Automobile

Automobile costs will follow the same basic calculations made previously but, if you have driven to work, you will now automatically eliminate this driving. Keep in mind, however, the rapidly escalating costs of running an automobile and do not underestimate them.

Retired persons often make a basic change in automobile usage and, therefore, in the annual cost. This may be possible if you foresee a substantial reduction in mileage. In addition to gasoline and oil, repairs and replacements are closely related to mileage. Depreciation is great in the early years but decreases rapidly with time. Insurance, licence, garage, etc. remain constant. The simple reduction of your mileage may make the annual running costs come to a very much smaller figure. If, for example, you now expect to cut your mileage in half, you could keep the car twice as long and your average annual depreciation would be much lower. This is calculated in detail in Chapter 4.

If you reduce your mileage to 5000 miles per year by eliminating that drive to work and keep your car twice as long, or until it has gone 50,000 miles (a ten-year period), your average depreciation would be reduced to perhaps $400, a saving of $500 per annum and your running expense to $344 from $688, a saving of $344. The total cost would then be $744 per year for this restricted mileage.

Your Total Expenses and What You Can Do to Change Them

Now total your expected expenses and compare them with the anticipated income. How does it look? Is your income adequate? If it is and you have listed all the things you wish to do, there is no problem. However, if there is not enough income to cover the expenses or if there are still things which you had hoped to be able to afford but which you did not include until you knew your position, you should now investigate the possible ways of increasing your income and reducing your expenditure, particularly on items which now provide little satisfaction. This is well worth very careful investigation because it may result in enabling you to undertake or have activities which, at first sight, appeared to be beyond your means. There are plenty of opportunities to make adjustments which are often painless.

You have arrived at the point where you should give serious consideration to making some basic changes in your life style, and you should have in mind your particular financial circumstances when you do so. By now, it must have occurred to you that you are going to be living a very different life. You will have many new needs, goals and desires.

Much of your pre-retirement life was designed to take care of your job and your family. Now these have gone. Many of your expenditures made for these purposes have continued on, but now you derive little satisfaction or value from them. It is time that you reviewed each one seriously and judged it by your new standard. Does it make a worthwhile contribution to the welfare and happiness of yourself and your spouse now that you are retired? You no longer must keep up appearances for your job and do those things that it often required. Everyone understands that retired people are on a lower income basis. It is accepted that there are different standards and that it is wise and prudent to consider cost and value more carefully. Those things related to "appearance," which seemed so important when fighting your way up and trying to establish a position for yourself and your family, can be forgotten. Relax, enjoy life and spend your money for true value.

Before reviewing your list again, give the matter some serious thought. Challenge every item and make each justify its retention on your list.

Preliminary Estimate of Living Expenses After Retirement

	Annual Total	Monthly Total
Income tax	$ 0	$ 0
Utilities	250	20.84
House	1301	108.42
Food	1250	104.16
Clothing	450	37.50
Appliances	50	4.17
Furniture	150	12.50
Personal care	100	8.33
Medical and health	175	14.58
Cigarettes and alcohol	250	20.84
Life insurance	162	13.50
Automobile (at reduced mileage)	744	62.00
Public transportation	75	6.25
Recreation	250	20.84
Personal spending (miscellaneous)	200	16.66
Gifts and donations	100	8.33
Total	$5507	$458.92

Note: No vacation is provided for.

This compares with an estimated gross annual income of $5,501.32 (Chapter 5) which will not cover the above expenses. Obviously some changes must be made. Therefore, let us examine the possibility of increasing your income.

The above is a minimum budget and it would be desirable to find extra income to provide for a vacation, emergencies and the extras which can add much interest to your life.

CHAPTER 7

HOW TO INCREASE YOUR RETIREMENT INCOME

There is an old saying that before thirty a girl needs looks, from thirty to sixty-five the woman needs clothes, and after sixty-five the old girl needs money! It sounds harsh, but there is one definite fact there for certain -- after sixty-five, money becomes increasingly necessary. There are more things which you must pay for and fewer which you can do yourself.

Retirement means the loss of your earnings from employment. It may be replaced, in part, by a pension related to employment but such is not generally the case for those retiring now. The usual sources of income have been discussed in Chapter 5 and it is only the rare person who has managed to arrive at retirement with as much income as he or she had while working. Most will find themselves in the position of our example, with income reduced below anticipated spending. No one wants a reduction of income or enjoys reducing expenditure. They can be the most important factors in the fear of retirement or the failure to enjoy it.

Fortunately, the shortage is usually relatively small and there are many possible ways of making it up. Perhaps you would enjoy adding many other activities at considerable cost. Why not? This is your time, so make a sincere effort to take advantage of the following suggestions for providing the funds to do so -- particularly those which will enable you to use the things which you toiled for and built up during your working years.

There are two possible ways in which you might increase your income. The first is by reviewing the manner in which your present capital is used and invested, and seeing if it can be re-employed to provide a greater net income. You have spent a lifetime in acquiring these assets. Now use them to the best possible advantage.

The second way is by finding employment, full- or part-time, to provide additional earnings. You will be the best judge of whether you have some saleable skill to offer -- generally, if you have reached sixty-five, a full-time job is very difficult to find. However, there may be part-time work available which you could enjoy.

If you want employment, remember that the best time to get a job is when you are still working. Employers think they are then obtaining the skill and experience of a valuable producing person -- a few months later, after retirement, they may view you as an entirely different person. Prior to retirement, try to locate the type of work and the actual job. If successful, you then start off with a known figure to add into the income side, rather than a hope. Be realistic and keep in mind that this can continue only for a restricted period and then age will finally catch up and you will be content with a more leisurely life.

It may be that instruction or training through a night course available at some local educational institution would improve your skills and make them much more valuable commercially. Look into this and get the training while still employed.

How do you go about increasing the income from all those things you own? Start off with a consideration of the manner in which your assets are employed, examining each carefully. Does each produce money income or, if it does not, does it provide a valuable satisfaction worth the value of the income it replaces? Look at your cash, investments, home, insurance and cottage to see if you are getting as much out of them as you should. How little income is earned by what is perhaps a considerable sum of valuable items may surprise you!

You may not realize how much you have accumulated in total assets during your career. Most of these assets were not obtained originally to produce income but to serve other purposes. Often their accumulation was a by-product of some other enterprise. Do you know how much they total? Have you calculated what this sum could do to increase your income if rearranged and invested with this purpose in mind?

First, see what you have to work with. List all your assets. Separate those belonging to husband and wife because this may be of importance from a tax standpoint.

Follow this check list.

Cash
Bank account
Life insurance cash value
Life insurance accumulated dividends
Stocks, bonds and investments
Objects of art and antiques
Investment property
Value of house
Value of cottage
Automobile
Other

How much do these total and how much are they earning for you? What can they earn? You can invest in chartered bank or trust company certificates of deposits or debentures. Many of these are guaranteed by the Canada Deposit Insurance Corporation up to a total of $20,000 for each investor in each company and these are considered a safe investment. Some are for a fixed term of one to five years and cannot be cashed before maturity. Others can be cashed at any time and generally bear a slightly lower rate of interest for this privilege. The rates on these vary with the general rate of interest from 8% to 10% (spring, 1974). So let us take 8% as our figure. This is not to say that they are recommended as the only or best investments, but they are used as an example of non-speculative investment and are obtainable almost everywhere without difficulty. Buy them at the counter of any bank or trust company. The manager will explain what his institution offers currently and this will give you a definite figure to work against. Multiply the value of your assets by 8%, or whatever rate is available at the time, and this is the possible income they could generate if all turned into cash and so invested. This step is not recommended; it is simply an exercise to alert you to the income these assets could generate should it be needed. Now let us examine these assets and some possible changes you might consider.

Cash, Chequing and Liquid Investments

First, let us consider how you use your cash. This is normally kept in bank or trust company accounts. It is there to serve two purposes -- firstly, as a reserve of money available to pay regular and perhaps unexpected expenses and, secondly, to generate as much interest income as possible. For most efficient use, establish what you require for regular monthly expenses. Keep one account for this purpose and have the necessary figure in it. Next, scrape all other cash sources together and look for maximum investment income from it.

Before deciding where to bank and how to invest, you must realize that not all banks and/or trust companies have the same charges for handling an account or pay the same interest rate on savings. Some charge for cheques, others offer free chequing privileges. There can be quite a difference in annual cost. Therefore, go to each of the banks and trust companies that are convenient and ask the manager to explain what accounts and services he offers, what the interest rates are and what he charges for. The important feature here is whether there is a charge for cheques. If there is a charge at all, look for an account for which there is no charge for chequing privileges. Have all surplus money, that is the surplus over the maximum figure required for monthly operation, invested in interest-bearing deposits or investments. Whether to charge for cheques or not is frequently left to the branch manager's discretion. If your overall business with the branch is worthwhile, and the number of cheques is reasonable, the manager may elect to forego a cheque charge. Offer the manager all your business, including investments, and see what he wishes to offer in return.

The number of cheques you issue can be controlled by the use of a credit card which enjoys widespread acceptance. It gives the convenience and economy of one cheque to cover many purchases at no extra cost. There is no charge provided payment is made by the prescribed date. The time lag between purchase and payment, often two months, leaves this money with you to earn interest for that time. If there are "specials" where such credit cards cannot be used, it is generally best to pay cash to take advantage of them.

While you are investigating the various accounts, ask about the branch's investment certificates or certificates of deposit and debentures or whatever name each has for longer term fixed income investments. Ascertain the following.

1. What lengths of contract are available (for example, one to five years)?

2. What is the rate of interest for each?

3. Are they cashable on request before maturity? (This is important.) Is there a penalty in interest for doing so?

4. Can these certificates be sold or assigned as security? (Some cannot, some can.) If so, and the money is needed before maturity, can the debenture be sold? (Some cannot.) There may be a small discount but at least the funds are available. Often the bank or trust company manager can sell them for you or sometimes they can be sold through a regular bond dealer or privately to a friend.

With this information, you are ready to make a decision. Remember that it is desirable to have some assets that can be readily converted into cash to meet emergencies in health, housing repairs, etc. It is probable that your best income and lowest expenses will be achieved by doing one of the following.

(a) Open an account on which no charge will be made for the cheques. The interest rate isn't important here because you plan to have the balance down very low.

(b) Investment the amount of emergency money you require in some sort of certificate or debenture, Canada Savings Bonds or other investment that can be cashed on demand and which yields the highest available interest rate.

(c) Put the balance in some high-yielding secure investment, preferably one or ones which can be sold or assigned at will.

This arrangement will maximize your earnings and decrease your expenses. More money will be made available if you use a broad coverage "no cost" credit card.

Next, it is very convenient to assign some assets to your bank or trust company as security so that you can issue a cheque at home or abroad for more than the cash in your account. Have it understood with the manager that, if you issue such a cheque, it will never be refused. He will automatically create a loan against your security and deposit it in your account to cover the cheque. (Loans against good securities are made at a lower rate of interest, too!) This serves two purposes -- supplying a convenient source of funds when quickly required and making available these funds without selling the security. The funds may be required only for a short time and it is more economical to pay the interest than to sell the security and then reinvest when the funds are again available. If the requirement is permanent and securities must be liquidated, time is provided to decide on the best course instead of forcing ill-considered action.

Before borrowing money, you should realize that the cost or interest rate will vary considerably depending on the organization from which you borrow and the security which you can give. If you go to a bank or trust company and borrow against bonds or their own certificate, you will get the lowest rate. The next rate, about 2% higher, will apply if you borrow on your name only. If you go to a finance company, the rates may be up to 12% or more higher! It will pay you to investigate and take advantage of the best opportunity.

How to Make the Most Income Now from Your Life Insurance

You bought life insurance in the first place to protect your family. The most important decision which you must make now is whether to cash the policy and employ the money in some other way or to keep the policy in force but take advantage of its provisions to earn income. Many do not realize that this can be done. Which is the better course will depend upon you and your personal circumstances and, as the provisions of policies vary greatly, on the terms of your particular policy. Is there someone for whom you should maintain all the financial protection possible if you die first? How important is current income compared with that future protection? Will a compromise which keeps the insurance in force and provides some income now be enough?

You have already determined your need for extra income; now consider the necessity of providing for any responsibility which you may have for a spouse, relative, or disabled child. Balance one factor against the other to reach a decision.

When you pass away, some sources of income stop at once, others may continue to provide specified but reduced benefits for certain survivors. Determine what these facts will be in your case. They are investigated more fully in Chapter 13 so will not be considered again here.

When you bought your insurance some years ago, you had a choice of many types of policies. When the salesman suggested that you buy standard insurance rather than "term," he probably pointed out certain possible future advantages of doing so. Standard policies build up an ever-increasing cash surrender value (C.S.V.) over the years while the term policies do not. The C.S.V. can be drawn as cash, used to purchase paid-up insurance, turned into an annuity or used as security for a loan. You have paid a higher premium to build up this C.S.V. It is a form of forced saving. This money is yours. Use it wisely now and it can transform your insurance from an expense into a source of income. To be sure that you know what your policy provides, read it now. It is a legal contract and sets out in detail exactly what it will do for you. The more common policies and their features are as follows.

(a) Term

It is written for a specific term of years, i.e. five, ten or fifteen, or perhaps until a certain age, then it terminates. You have no insurance beyond that date and it very rarely goes beyond sixty-five years of age.

It has no cash surrender value, but most term policies contain the right to change them into a standard policy at the going rate for your age and sex without medical examination, up to a certain date.

This is likely to be the only decision you can make respecting term at this time.

(b) Endowment

This policy is written to terminate at a certain date at which point the face value is paid to the beneficiary and no further premiums are payable. It is usually written to provide a sum of money at a certain age for a specific purpose such as a college education, a home or retirement.

(c) Whole Life

This is insurance that will carry on until death at which time the face value of the policy, plus any dividends which may have accumulated and less any loans against it, will be paid to the beneficiary. One of the problems now is that you continue to pay the same premiums all through retirement. This is one of the expenses that you may be able to eliminate as shown below.

There are three common types of policy.

(d) Participating

Participating insurance means that the policy participates and shares in the company's earnings and you receive your share of them through policy dividends, usually allotted annually. You can elect to have those dividends accumulate and the company pay interest on the accumulated value, or you can draw them as cash or have them deducted from the annual premium payable to reduce it. While term insurance generally earns dividends, these usually must be drawn annually and not accumulated.

(e) Non-Participating

This policy, in contrast to the previous one, does not participate in the company's profits and earns no dividends.

(f) Life with Premiums Payable for a Specified Term

These policies are generally referred to as a "20 pay," "30 pay," life or any other specified term of years and mean that you pay premiums for that number of years only. The policy then continues in force until death or until some other option is exercised.

When you read your policy, be sure that you understand which of the above types it is, and not only what further obligation you have to it, but what it can do to provide income for you now.

If it is a term policy, the only possible options are to convert to a standard policy, let it run to its termination or cancel it. For all other policies, determine first whether you have to continue payment of premiums for life, or if it is a policy for which premium payment terminates at a certain date.

(g) Dividends

The annual dividend for a participating policy will not be shown in any policy as it is not a guaranteed feature. Its amount is not known until the company has calculated its profits and decided on the amount payable each year. You will, therefore, receive an annual statement showing the dividend allotted for the year plus any accumulation from prior years.

If you have permitted dividends to accumulate, there is only one recommended course -- draw them now and invest the money in secure investments such as those previously discussed. They will probably earn at least 3% more interest than paid by the insurance company.

Your Possible Options

(a) Exchange for Paid-Up Insurance

Your present policy can be exchanged for a paid-up policy of a lower face value without your having to pay further premiums. The size of the new policy will depend on your age at the date of exchange and will be shown in the policy. Check to see if you have the option of a participating or non-participating policy. In our example (page 59), a $10,000 policy can be exchanged for a new $7,570 paid-up participating policy.

In this case, the insured retains a policy of about 75% of the original. No further premiums are payable and, as it is a participating policy, annual dividends of about $100 per year can be expected after the first year.

(b) Cash Surrender Value

Every policy other than term will show a cash surrender value for specified dates over the life of the policy. If it does not show one for the approximate date on which you are examining the policy, the company will provide this for you on request. The C.S.V. is the amount that is payable if the policy is cancelled and no longer exists as insurance. This can be done at any time and you can do whatever you wish with the money. The policy offers only two choices aside from taking the cash or paid-up insurance. First, you may use the proceeds to buy an annuity and the policy sets the prices at which the company guarantees to sell you certain types of annuities. This is of very little value in most cases today because the old cost of annuity is much higher than the current one and you would probably be unwise to purchase at the prices shown. Therefore, the company will usually sell you an annuity at a lower price than that specified so, if you wish to consider one, ask for the current rates. The second option is to leave the money on deposit at interest. The insurance company rate is generally below that of other sound investments so you will probably wish to make your own investment if you choose not to purchase an annuity.

(c) Annuities

Annuities are popular investments for retired persons because they provide worry-free income. Almost any combination of features is available and each contract sets them out specifically. Understand first what your needs are and be sure that any contract you purchase is clear to you and provides for your needs. It should specify whether the annuity is for a definite term or for life, and if it is based only on the one life. It may be a "joint annuity," in which case it pays perhaps the purchaser and another beneficiary as long as either one survives. It should indicate what happens when the first beneficiary dies. Does the second continue to receive the full or a reduced amount? Some provide payment for a guaranteed number of years and payment to a third beneficiary in case the originals die quickly. The cost will vary with the provisions for payment. Selection of the most suitable one for you may require some study. Not every insurance company charges the same price for similar contracts. You are free to shop around, ask prices from several companies and buy where you receive the best value.

Annuities have major drawbacks. They are expensive and eat up the capital. The company has to charge for investing the money and administering the contract and this is much more costly than generally realized. If you are competent to make suitable investments or have someone you trust who can, perhaps a son or daughter or advisor, you may be much better off to invest the money yourself. Remember that the monthly cheque received from an annuity is a combination of two things -- earned interest and return of capital. When the annuity finally terminates, the capital has been completely used up. There is nothing left for your estate. Contrast this with the investment of the C.S.V. discussed below. Would you like to retain the capital to leave to someone?

Annuity payments coming from an annuity purchased with capital on which income tax has been paid when earned, usually are not taxed in full; only the interest portion is liable. An annuity purchased with the proceeds of life insurance would probably so classify while one purchased with the proceeds from a registered retirement savings plan would not. If you plan to purchase either, check for current regulations and classification of your proposed plan.

(d) Investment of the C.S.V.

You may cancel the policy, take the C.S.V. and invest the money suggested above thereby having almost as great an annual income (or an even greater one) with the capital remaining intact! In the example set out on page 59, the C.S.V. of $4,999 would purchase an annuity as described of $480 per year. If the money was invested at 8%, this would bring an annual income of $399.92, if at 10%, an income of $499.90, actually larger, and in both cases the capital would remain intact!

(e) Borrow the Cash Surrender Value and Invest at a Profit!

It is not necessary to cancel the policy to use the C.S.V. to earn you an income. A policy usually specifies that the policy holder can demand a loan of the cash surrender value of the policy, less one year's interest payments. The rate of interest to be charged is set and, in most of the older policies that we will now be considering, it will be 6%. This means that the C.S.V. could be borrowed at 6% and reinvested at the going interest rate. The difference of perhaps 2% to 4% would be clear income. In the case of the policy shown as an example, the loan of $4,471 would produce a net income of $89.52 at 8% or $179.04 at 10%. This, together with the annual dividend, would enable you to continue to carry your insurance in force, retaining it for your spouse, dependants or heirs. Instead of the expense of paying the premiums out of income, it would provide a net cash profit for current spending!

Your Decision

If you have life insurance, you must now make an important decision. Such a step should be made only after careful consideration and with a full understanding of the facts. Once made, it may be final, and you can't change your mind. Don't let one person, particularly the agent, talk you into some course of action. Look into the alternatives and discuss them with your spouse and trusted advisors.

Balance the facts. Protect those for whom the insurance was purchased to protect, and then use it to give the balance of present income and future increase in your estate which you consider desirable.

Cost of Annuities

One company quotes as follows for a male aged sixty-five. For each $1,000 invested, the annuity pays $9.25 per month or $110.76 per year for life. This guarantees payment for ten years and, if the beneficiary dies in less than ten years, receipt of payment by some other designated beneficiary for the balance of the period.

Joint Annuity

If a husband and wife are both sixty-five and an annuity is purchased to continue payment as long as either one is alive, $1,000 would purchase $8.01 per month or $96.12 per year.

Review of an Actual Policy

Whole Life Participating Insurance
Face value: $10,000
Date of issue: January, 1939
Annual premium: $163
Current dividend: $142
Net premium cost 1974: $21.20
Options:
1. Exchange for a paid-up participating policy worth $7,570 and receive an annual dividend estimated at $100.

2. Surrender the policy for $4,999 and invest the money or purchase an annuity.

3. Borrow $4,471 against C.S.V. at 6% and reinvest at a higher current rate.

4. If dividends have been allowed to accumulate, withdraw
    the total amount of $4,757.20 now and invest at 8%. The
    yield will be $380.57. At 10% it would be $475.72. This
    is an addition to other income changes.

Results of Various Options Listed Above

Option Number

1. (a) Premiums are no longer payable.
    (b) There is a dividend income of, perhaps, $100.
    (c) An insurance of $7,570 remains in force.

2. (a) Investment at 8% yields an income of $399.92
    (b) Investment at 10% yields an income of $499.90
    (c) No further life insurance is in force.
    (d) Capital remains intact.

3. (a) Cost of borrowing $4,471 at 6% $268.26
         Cost of annual premium $163.20
         Total $431.46

         Reduction in costs by annual dividend $142.00
         Therefore, combined cost of policy
           and loan $289.46

    (b) Investment at 8% yields an income of $357.68
         and a profit of $ 66.23

    (c) Investment at 10% yields an income of $447.10
         and a profit of $138.54

    (d) Insurance of $10,000 remains in force and, as
         long as it does, the C.S.V. will increase by ap-
         proximately $169 per year. Remember, at death,
         any loan outstanding will be deducted from the
         face value of the policy when paid.

Objects of Art, Antiques, Etc.

You may be surprised how much some of the things you own are worth. Don't dispose of them without determining their value. How often have you walked by an antique shop and seen old crockery, equipment and furniture displayed at substantial prices and similar to something which you or your family threw out not so long ago? Even items you know to be valuable may have increased more than you realize. How about those pictures? Who is the artist? One man suddenly discovered three paintings by one of the "Group of Seven" artists in his family's basement! You have two alternatives if you have old items which have now become valuable -- sell them and invest the proceeds or hold them and let them continue to increase in value. Your decision will probably depend on your present need for cash compared with your hope of obtaining a higher value in the future.

Your House or Cottage

If you own either or both of these, and a condominium or co-op apartment would be included in the classification, these are probably the most valuable assets which you have. Look at each one separately. They were perhaps purchased some time ago under different circumstances, to fill a very different need. They were probably bought when you had children living at home. Is either of them suitable for you now in retirement, or would you be better served with another? Perhaps your house is too big, has a high cash value, expensive taxes, heat and maintenance. Something different might be more suitable today; should you consider making a move? Later on, in Chapter 15, we go into alternative types of housing suitable for retired persons and reading that chapter may help you decide if you should change and which type of accommodation you should select. However, here the basic economics can be considered.

Most persons, by the time of retirement, have paid off the mortgage on the family home. While values of houses will vary widely with the location and type of individual home, they will be relative to others in the same area. In other words, a larger home will be much more valuable than a comparable smaller one in the same district and, if houses sell at lower prices in your area, apartments will also be rented at lower prices. Let us take an example to illustrate what you might do. Have your home valued, preferably by three agents. It is probably worth more than you think today. Don't guess. Next, investigate the costs of the alternative type of dwelling you wish to consider. Say, for example, this was a home selling for $45,000. The real estate commission, legal fees, costs of moving and extra purchases necessary for the new home probably would take close to $5,000. This would leave available a net sum of $40,000. The next thing would be for you to decide how much this was worth to you. So you would go back to the rate which you decided you would accept on an investment. If it was 10%, your annual income would be $4,000. Now your home had a cost for taxes, heat, mortgage interest, insurance, repairs and maintenance calculated earlier (page 28) to be $1,301, so you would save this expense and have an income of $4,000 -- a combined total of $5,301. There would be income tax on your $4,000 income, so you would look up your rate and deduct it. Suppose it was $895 -- you would still have $4,406 to provide a place to live. Any lower cost would mean that much extra cash for other purposes.

If, however, you like your house and the neighbourhood and would prefer to remain, but you have too much space, perhaps you can turn this disadvantage into a source of revenue and continue to live there. Have an architect or builder look it over. You may remodel and come out with a duplex, providing ideal accommodation for yourselves as well as a rentable apartment to produce the extra revenue you desire. Before going too far, check the local building restrictions to see if this is permissible.

If you do not have the ready cash to pay for alterations, this would be an excellent use for any accumulated insurance dividends or a policy loan. Some provinces guarantee low-rate bank loans for this purpose and municipalities often give special tax treatment. If it looks like an acceptable possibility, look into it. Your bank manager will know the details of special loans available.

As a fringe benefit, you might be able to rent to a younger person who could look after the snow clearing, gardening, etc., and be a built-in helper when needed.

What, then, are your alternatives?

1.   Renting an apartment at, say, $200 per month,
     which would leave you with your accommodation
     paid and $2,006 more cash than you had before.

2.   Buying a condominium or co-op apartment.

3.   Buying a mobile home.

4.   Buying a smaller house. Here the savings would
     depend on your success in buying one at a suffi-
     ciently lower price to leave an important cash
     difference after everything is paid and on the lower
     operating costs of a smaller place. The most like-
     ly worthwhile difference would occur if you moved
     from an expensive city area to a town where the
     cost price of the property, taxes and maintenance
     are lower. Such a move could make significant
     contribution to your income and ease the strain.

Your cottage, if you wish, can be regarded in exactly
the same manner and, after consideration, you may decide
upon a change. However, a cottage has an additional advantage because, if you desire, it can be rented for part of the
season and used by you for the balance of the time. The rent
might pay for the carrying costs and be all the assistance you
require. If owning a cottage gives you a lot of satisfaction,
it's your right to try to arrange your affairs so that you can
keep it. On the other hand, cottages are selling at very high
prices in many areas. The sale of one might provide a substantial investment income which could mean a lot to you
now. Such income might provide you both with a resort holiday or a trip you would enjoy and still leave a chunk of cash
for other uses. Look into it and come up with the decision
that is most pleasing to you and your spouse.

What Should You Do?

When you made your initial listing of expected post-
retirement income and expenses, you found either adequate
income to continue on or a shortage. After examining the
various changes which could possibly be made in the income

63

side through reusing the assets you have, you are now in a position to decide. You can attack from either the income or the expenditure side, or a combination of both. Now, however, you have the knowledge of what can be done by reusing your assets for better financial return. Perhaps you see clearly changes which you want to make on the income side and which will solve any financial problem. If so, well and good. If not, there is still the other side. Consider each expenditure. Is it worth it now? Would you derive greater satisfaction if the money were spent in another way? Even if not a necessity, such an examination might result in more satisfaction, so why not do it? Later on, after you have given more consideration to the use of time, you will no doubt again revise your decisions.

Revised Possible Retirement Income
After Re-employing Assets

Life Insurance
If you draw the accumulated dividends of $4,757 and invested at 10%, you would have an income of $475.70.

Cash Surrender Value
By borrowing $4,471 against C.S.V. at 6% and reinvesting at 10%, your net income plus your saving on the annual premium would be $138.54.

Cancellation of Insurance Policy
If you cancel the policy, take the C.S.V. of $4,999 and invest at 10%, your annual income would be $499.90 plus your saving of $21.20 on the premium, giving a total of $521.10

or

If you buy a joint annuity (page 59) yielding $480 per annum, the premium saved would be $21.20, totalling $501.20.

Sale of Automobile and Investment

Income from investing $3,000 value at 10%	$ 300
Operating costs (as per budget)	$ 744
Total	$1,044

Cost of public transportation	$425
Net income	$619

(You save by using public transportation.)

64

House

Sale price of home	$45,000
Expenses	$ 5,000
Net for investing	$40,000

Income from investing at 10%	$ 4,000
Saving in operating cost of house	$ 1,301
Net saving and income	$ 5,301

Cost of renting an apartment	$2,400
Income tax on investment	$ 895
Total costs	$3,295

Net increase in income after apartment is paid is $2,006.

The total possible increase in income over expenses if you carried out the suggestions above could be as follows.

Income from cashing life insurance policy and investing proceeds	$ 499.90
Saving in net annual insurance premiums	21.20
Giving up car for public transportation	619.00
Selling home and renting apartment	2,006.00
Increased Income	$3,109.10

The deficiency in income shown in Chapter 6, page 45 was $37. This leaves a surplus of $3072.10 available for further discretionary spending. You may decide to implement only sufficient of the above suggestions to provide the income change you require. On the other hand, you may choose to implement them all and enjoy extensive travelling or a winter vacation. The choice is yours.

The above items are not the only ways in which income can be increased or expenses reduced. There is still the possibility of full- or part-time employment, rental of rooms, etc. What they do is illustrate the many possibilities of working out a satisfactory financial plan.

CHAPTER 8

THE USE OF TIME

Before one is faced with imminent retirement, the thought of having unlimited time at one's disposal seems like Utopia. However, unless you have prepared for it, when retirement arrives it is not as delightful as you thought it would be.

You are so conditioned to working full days, generally against a time schedule, that subconsciously your mind will expect to continue. For years you have striven to arrive on time, complete jobs on time, keep appointments and do so much per hour. Regardless of what your employment was, time was a steady master and you were the puppet on its strings. Nice as it might seem to be released from this bondage, it is still keeping its hold on your mind. Subconsciously you feel that there must be something you should be doing, somewhere you should be going and the guilty feeling that you are forgetting something lingers on. The change is so sudden that it is difficult to relax and enjoy this new-found freedom.

There is no statement respecting the use of time that will apply to everyone. People are individuals and no two are exactly alike. Some require what amounts to an almost frenzied schedule, even in retirement, while at the opposite end of the scale others will be fully satisfied with the rocking chair, pipe and slippers. This is the reason that it has been constantly emphasized that you must understand **your** needs and build a programme that fills **your** personal requirements. Whatever it is will be perfectly normal for you. With this explanation, adjust the following remarks to suit you and do not feel that there must be something wrong if the characteristics described do not fit in with your personality.

You have been taught that you must work to live and it is difficult to believe that those cheques will still come if you don't. You feel somewhat like a kid playing hooky, or a soldier absent without leave. Those ingrained feelings about work and time combine to make it difficult to slow down, relax and enjoy.

Many do not find the employment of their time an easy thing to accomplish. Previously you have had only the evening, weekends and annual vacation at your disposal. These were not difficult to use; on the contrary, they were awaited with pleasure and were generally necessary for you to get many of your chores done. There was only a little time, perhaps a few hours, left to loaf and enjoy. The annual vacation was anticipated as an opportunity to either stay at home and do those things which had had to wait for a longer period of time to be available, or it was used for a trip away from home. If there were children, these holidays were a very special occasion. There has been no problem with leisure time until now. Once you have retired, time is a totally new experience and leisure time is no longer eagerly awaited. It becomes a steady procession of days, weeks and years with virtually no demands upon you. The chores are soon caught up, the vacation trips taken and the days still come. Unless you find useful things with which to fill them, they are empty and boredom sets in. The one who spoke of "doing a little gardening" or "travelling" when questioned about his or her plans, finds that these fill only a few days in certain seasons and, that, when these are over, the days continue to come in a steady, boring procession.

Is there an answer to this problem? Certainly there is; anyone who thinks that there is nothing to do lacks imagination. There are so many interesting and available things.

Think for a moment about time and how your valuation of it has changed over the years. As a young person you considered it as almost a renewable resource. There was an unending supply, or so it seemed at that point, and old age was so far away. If you made a mistake or failed in some endeavour, there was always time to try again. Your dreams were all still possible but, as the years went by, there were more candles on the birthday cake and, at some point, certain things turned out to be final. There would not be another chance. Patterns unlikely to be reversible developed and limitations became evident. Time began to take on greater value.

Frequently, events of a serious nature drive it home -- the passing of friends and contemporaries, greying hair, illnesses, the children's growth. One event that has great power to force an evaluation of your use of time, a change of plans, goals and the direction of your life is a serious illness or major surgery. It brings the realization that, as this has happened to you once, it probably will again. There is always a percentage of terminal risk involved, however small, and it could happen to you. Those long days in hospital, perhaps in an almost helpless state, give rise to serious thoughts which have not occurred to you before. Frequently we are told by someone emerging from such an experience that he or she has now changed plans for the future. New standards of value will be used to judge the alternatives. These are down-to-earth with no fooling involved. There will be no more time wasted on trivialities.

Retirement is a similar experience. It is like turning off a crowded high-speed freeway on to an unpaved country road. No longer must you strain to keep your place and watch the traffic. The tension fades away, you slow down. There is still much time, but it is not endless. Many avenues are now closed, but many new ones are opened. These are largely related to the fact that your days are now entirely at your disposal and you will be able to do so much more because of this. The real pity is to see a person who fails to use it well, and lets it fritter away. There will be no "try overs" now. This is the last time around. The important thing is to accomplish the aim which was decided upon earlier -- to promote the greatest satisfaction for you and your spouse.

Do not let the strangeness of the new situation drug you into inactivity, as it does with so many persons. There is very general agreement amongst doctors that the one who, on retirement, fades out of an active life and loses interest, simply succumbs to the boredom, frustration and depression which results and dies in a relatively short time. Make the effort, force yourself if necessary, but get out and get started.

How Do You Make Your Plans?

First, make a list of all the things which you have often thought you would like to do.

Now continue to think of new things you might like to investigate. Bring your spouse in on this session and have his or her wishes added in. Keep in mind our earlier warning that retirement is a united rather than a solo effort. Put everything down. Don't omit anything because you think it is too expensive, too unusual, that others might laugh or that it might be beyond your ability. The only real reasons to leave anything out at this point would be because it is illegal, immoral or it strongly offends your spouse and would be a source of constant irritation. This is important to avoid. You really don't know, for example, if something is too expensive until you make the final decisions respecting how you will spend your income. You may give something else up or get the money you need from one of those new sources of income discussed in Chapter 7. There may be a relatively cheap way to accomplish what you want now that you are retired. Perhaps there are discounts for retired persons or, at certain time, lower prices which can now be enjoyed. Put everything on your list for you might wish to sacrifice something of a lower priority in order to be able to enjoy a high-priority activity.

High priority, that's the goal now. Once you have the list of interests, it will become apparent that you can't have them all. Think about them and assign an order of preference. Decide which you want most, that's number one, and so on down the line.

The big shock, and it is frequently referred to and recognized as "retirement shock," is caused by the termination of your job. Therefore, it is necessary to find not a substitute, because that infers that it will be inferior, but something new and hopefully more desirable to fill the gap that the job left. You probably have never analyzed what your job did for you other than demand your days and provide the pay cheque. Now is the time to see what it did provide. List all those things which you enjoyed about it on one side. You will want to equal these in your new list. On the other side, put down all those things you did not like. Now your goal will be to eliminate these.

There are some things which you may not have realized were important for you. The first is a sense of belonging. It is a natural desire to be an accepted member of a group and, to a greater degree than realized, a job fills this need. It is one of the things which becomes obvious very quickly after retirement. The second is the sense of achievement which a job brings and this, again, has important psychological weight. The person who has risen to a position of authority may have derived much of his job satisfaction from exercising it. The workman who has learned and taken pride in his skill, and who has done his job well, has drawn his compensation from its use. Listen to the first man when he is discussing his position, and it soon becomes obvious, Watch the skilled workman perform and see the satisfaction shine through when he competently performs some function that has required his special skill. Both derive much satisfaction from the recognition which they receive for the skill displayed in the performance of their jobs. They may mistakenly assume that the recognition is of them as persons and belongs to them. But, when they retire, they find that it was not. It was a part of the job and was loaned to them only while they had those jobs. On leaving, it was handed to their successors. They feel naked without it and need something of a similar nature to take its place. Both the need for belonging and achieving, therefore, should be on your list of wants requiring satisfaction.

This list may include a great many untried things. It is not, however, final. In most cases, any one can be tried and dropped if not satisfactory. The main thing is to get started, weed out those which you do not enjoy, although they often point the way to other interests that do provide the fulfillment you seek.

This is one of the reasons for starting preparation for retirement years in advance if possible -- by doing so, the fumbling and problems of the initial retirement period will be eliminated. You will have the best possible start. Instead of retiring **from** something, you will be retiring **to** something you enjoy and there is a world of difference between the two!

If you have not done this and are now in retirement, it's never too late to start. As a matter of fact, with all the

71

free time, you will get results more quickly and your actual needs will no longer be guesses; they will be staring you in the face.

After beginning by listing the things which come to mind, read over some of the possible activities which follow. There may be some new ideas of real interest for you.

Join the Club

A very important and helpful move is to join a senior citizens' group or club. They are almost everywhere. If there is not one nearby, find a few other people who qualify and start your own. Established groups are located in almost every place of worship, regardless of the denomination. They are merely service groups organized to be of benefit to anyone wishing to join and have no religious requirements or goals. You do not need to be a member of that particular religious group to belong and you should not hesitate to join if you are a non-member. The YMCA, some municipalities and other interested organizations also sponsor them. If there are several clubs available near your home, talk to some of the members of each club before joining one. You would be well advised to attend a meeting of each to enable you to join the one which seems to have the most compatible membership and enjoyable activities for you.

The great value in such a group is, firstly, that its members will have aims identical to yours and, secondly, there will be many persons who will be a real source of assistance and information. You will make new friends. They can advise you of the opportunities of particular interest to senior citizens. Many local organizations give special treatment to them. There is such a multitude of these things which, often, are not well advertised. There are very many activities, trips, special vacation plans, etc., of which you might not otherwise hear. You will be welcome in such a group. Most are looking for more members, for the larger the group the easier it is to get enough people to stage a special event requiring, for example, a chartered bus. Many of the members will also be looking for new friends with similar interests. They will be very happy to tell you all they know about the opportunities discussed in this book and show you how and where to apply. If you want activities, they will know where they can be found in a form best suited to senior citizens. They will be happy to introduce you and often teach and train you, if necessary. Such contacts are of real value. Many persons have found that their greatest pleasures are things which they would not have thought possible had such acquaintances not shown them the way. Many of their best friends are those whom they met through these groups.

In addition, the group members organize many interesting activities. You name it, some group somewhere probably does it. Many have formed bands or orchestras which don't make the big time but often appear on television and everyone seems to be having a great time. Most never played an instrument before, but they soon learn to play some simple one which lets them join in.

Such an activity might not be of interest to you. This only emphasizes the importance of selecting a suitable group. If your club consists of persons with similar backgrounds, interests and means, their plans will probably please you. Suitable entertainments for your group may be bus trips to the country in the autumn to enjoy the colours, a trip to a nearby city to see a show, shop or participate in other pleasing activities. When the bus can be chartered, it is more fun because it is fully occupied by your group, it can leave from your chosen point of departure and go direct to your destination. The fare is low and group rates are often available for meals and entertainment. You get a lot for your money and have good companionship with it.

Get Out and Be Seen!

Another thing you must do is get exposed. Go out, see others and be seen. You are no longer where the action is, so if you stay home you will be forgotten. Out of sight, out of mind. No one will call and the opportunities which you might have enjoyed pass without your knowing of their existence. You must find and join in with the appropriate group. Use every opportunity to meet people. Church services, church-sponsored or other community entertainments, sporting events, ratepayers meetings, the senior citizens' club, etc.

Even just walk around the neighbourhood and stop and talk to others who might appear to be of interest. It is amazing how simple contacts often lead to many unthought-of opportunities.

If you are asked to undertake some volunteer job, take it, or at least agree to give it a try. It may not be what you want but it could lead to one you do. Above all, beat boredom and find activities by getting out and making contacts. Do so at every opportunity.

You will find that your new friends will be a lot of help and will be needed, not only because they can introduce you to the retired way of life, but because they will replace many of your friends who are still working. Those who work are going to have much less free time than you have. They will spend it doing things required of them. You will have plenty of free time to be used when they are at work. Other retired persons will be better able to join you at such times.

Work It Out With Your Partner

At retirement, couples have a problem of their own. In those years when either or both partners were employed outside the home, they went their separate ways during working hours. It was a welcome change to be together during their leisure time.

Often their jobs developed different approaches and attitudes towards work, its performance and the way in which it should be organized. Now, when neither goes out to work, it is possible that the couple may spend all their time and take all their meals together. One partner may monopolize the time of the other. The division of the household work may become a problem if one partner feels that his or her method is superior. Partners may resent taking orders or giving in to each other, even though they willingly did so in the established rank system in paid employment. Often courtesies which would be granted to an outsider are neglected. It is common for friction to develop for these reasons, and occurs because the couple spend so much time together and rely on each other more than ever.

Avoid this friction, for a pleasant relationship will be important for happiness. Each must be willing to defer to a partner's strongly held view or to modify it to a mutually acceptable level. Each partner must realize that he or she can't win them all and be prepared to share in giving in on a fair basis. Because people are involved, it is not as easy as it should be, but success in attaining a mutually acceptable compromise is a worthwhile goal.

It was pointed out earlier that it will be much more enjoyable to live with a happy mate than one in a constant state of resentment and tension.

Many retired couples find it simple to divide up the work at home. Just what this division is will depend on the tasks to be done and the likes and dislikes of each partner. Divide the jobs up on a mutually satisfactory basis. Give each person an area of sole responsibility if desired and let the other stay out of it. This may mean that the husband has a workshop or area of his own which he can maintain to **his** standard of neatness. And he has a right to his standard in his corner, in return for giving his wife the same right in hers. Both should have their own way and neither should be asked to change.

It isn't necessary to plan all of every day but certain times should be set aside for use by each as desired or for specific activities on a regular basis.

Both partners have a right to a personal allowance which can be spent without permission from the other. This is a new freedom for some women, but now your government will make it possible for many who have not enjoyed this privilege. Everyone, regardless of sex or marital status, gets the Old Age Security Pension and, also, the Canada Pension, if he or she meets the qualifications and is eligible. Cheques will be in the name of the entitled person only and can be cashed by no one else without that person's endorsement.

Who Are You?

That is simple to answer if the enquirer merely seeks your name. But, if the question requires a more specific description of you and your characteristics, abilities and shortcomings, the answer is likely to be a long one. Further, there is not going to be agreement, for you will see yourself very differently from the way others will. Whether you downgrade or elevate yourself will depend on your personality, not your mirror. Yet, if you are to plan properly, it is necessary for you to know yourself and understand the things you need to have for a contented retirement.

Your spouse, family and close friends can often help but their opinions are biased because they expect you to react as they do and to like what they like. Perhaps you won't. So, while you invite and consider their criticism and suggestions, you must evaluate them for yourself and come up with your own image to guide you, the one that is the real you, not the one which you show the world. This will help you in selecting the proper package of activities and interests for your satisfaction.

Think about the people you know and you will be able to classify them as aggressive, shy, leaders, followers, etc. Decide where you fit in. If you are an aggressive leader, you will find no difficulty in breaking into any group or organization. If, on the other hand, you are the shy type, you may have difficulty at first but once in the group you will quietly fit in, making an unobtrusive contribution and enjoy it as much as anyone. In this case, you should attach yourself to a leader who will be happy to have you as a follower because he or she must have followers. This is one of the values of joining the senior citizens' group, a church club, the "Y" or any group where you are welcomed and drawn in without any aggressive act on your part.

There are so many different persons with different needs including physical action, creative work, reading, social activity, quiet times alone and contribution to the welfare of others. Think about this and select a pattern of things which will meet your needs and earn you contentment and happiness.

You no doubt have some activities in mind. How many more are you going to need? Start out by planning a week at a time. What activities do you already have that will continue -- regular meetings, perhaps church, social activities, sports? Put them in their places and start off to think about each day. You will be able to have a more leisurely breakfast than when you were getting off to work and then you may have decided to do certain household chores at that time. After that, how will you occupy the balance of the day with activities that will satisfy your needs and interest? Seek them out. Do not commit yourself irrevocably, if possible, to those which are untried for they may not be as interesting as you hoped. However, if they are not, participation often opens up new connections not previously considered and you may be able to move on to these and find even greater satisfaction.

To assist you in making your selections, read the suggestions in the following chapter. In addition, it will be very helpful if you can become interested in some hobby which you do yourself, at home, and which is not dependent on time, weather or strength. Something such as painting or woodworking would be ideal because these can be used to fill in days or parts of days for which no other activity is available, or when some plan has had to be cancelled.

CHAPTER 9

CHOOSE FROM THESE ACTIVITIES

Team Sports

(a) Curling

After retirement, you are likely to find most team sports too strenuous for your participation. There is one notable exception, however, made to order for Canadian winters -- curling. Facilities are available nearly everywhere. It is the ideal sport for retired men and women in that it is readily available, need not be expensive and can be practised either by team members in a competive schedule or by occasional players participating as desired. Young people work physically hard at the sweeping, older groups leave it to the individual to decide how hard he or she wishes to work. Many curl on into their eighties and some with physical disabilities are quite able to participate. There is no real work in throwing the stone. It is simply raised from the ice, swung slowly as a pendulum and released to allow its weight to carry it a long distance on the smooth ice.

Everyone is welcome. There is a place on each team for the inexperienced player as the "lead." Such persons are usually in short supply and the more experienced or expert players expect and welcome them. The real aim of the game at this stage of life is social, so there is no pressure to win as there is in the leagues of younger players. There are times for men or women only as well as mixed games in which husband and wife can both participate. Start at any age; someone will be glad to teach you.

An added bonus is the number of people you will meet. There are eight persons in every game and, in the mix of teams against whom you play, plus the changing personnel in "draw" or "choose-up" game, you will be constantly playing with and meeting new people. In the "draw" game, each person who wishes to play puts his or her name tag into a pot. Names are then drawn out at random to form teams. Often there is a small prize for the winners. Everyone accepts the other members of the team and makes them welcome regardless of their skill or lack of it. One thing that is very noticeable to the newcomer to curling is the courtesy shown to all and the desire to make the game a pleasant experience. There is little criticizing and no one is expected to "make" all his shots. Everyone is welcome except a complainer.

Do not hesitate to try curling if you have not done so. You will probably have friends who know of ice where there is curling. In any such place there is sure to be a group of retired people who play afternoons or mornings. If you do not know of one, look up the local arenas and hockey rinks and ask about curling. There is sure to be a nearby group that will welcome you.

(b) Hunting

This may not be thought of as a team sport but it may require membership in a group. This is so if you want to go on a "hunt" with a "club" who own a camp. Many people have often wished to participate in hunting but never had the time. Now, for you, this is no obstacle. To find a group, enquire amongst friends. Join an association of anglers and hunters, go to the meetings and you will make contacts. Join a gun club. Most groups need replacements from time to time. You don't need to be an expert shot. If you miss, you don't let anyone else down and the animal or bird will appreciate it. So don't hesitate to participate. You may enjoy local hunting near home, going out by the day alone or with friends. If you don't know the rules of your province, call on a sporting goods store or inquire at a local anglers' and hunters' association. There you can find information respecting seasons, open and closed areas, licence requirements, etc.

Individual Sports

These are of more interest now because there is no competition and you can go at your own pace. No one else relies on your skill to help him or her win or to be an interesting opponent to make the game worthwhile.

(a) Winter Sports

While not everyone will be able to ski after retirement, two developments in recent years have broadened the opportunities for participation at a level of exertion which you can meet. Firstly, the lifts have eliminated the hard work of climbing. Hills are graded and marked with respect to the degree of skill and effort required and you may select the easier slopes within your ability. Secondly, the return to fashion of cross-country skiing opens new vistas. This can be much less demanding physically and financially and there is little danger of serious accident. It simply involves trekking through the country on skis and is mostly done on trails that have been cleared. Often the snow is groomed and kept free of ruts and bare spots. There may be slopes and hills included but usually this type of trail avoids steep areas. Trails are now usually graded for degree of difficulty and are well marked. Provided you are not too cocky in the appraisal of your skill, you can select a suitable trail, enjoy the outing and come back to the starting point on your skis, not a stretcher. It is a very pleasing thing to see older persons skiing on a bright winter day, doing it their way and enjoying themselves as much as the younger ones.

(b) Snowmobiling

Snowmobiling is another recent development in sport and suitable for your participation. This activity has mushroomed rapidly and gained such widespread acceptance that it must appeal to most persons. It makes trips through snowbound winter woods a delightful event and it has made cottages not previously reachable in winter easily accessible and useable throughout the year.

There are areas, public and private, with cut and groomed trails and machines available for rental. The snowmobile has made it possible for many to get out and enjoy particularly the more inaccessible resort areas in the winter.

Summer Sports

(a) Golf

Summer provides the opportunity for a much broader range of sports, one of the most popular being golf. There are courses of all kinds, varying in degrees of physical effort required, expense and skill.

One of the recent developments is the "executive" course. It is much shorter with holes running about half the length of those on a regular course. They are generally less challenging. "Challenging" flashes a quick warning to the knowledgeable. When applied to a golf course it means that it is so difficult, with water traps, extra deep bunkers, forests, etc., that it drives even the winners of the "Masters' Tournaments" over the brink. Such a course is no place for a duffer. It is needed by the better players to keep their games from becoming routine. Now the "executive" courses fill the need for those who lack the skill to handle the challenging course and the stamina to play eighteen full-length holes. It is made to order for the non-expert retired couple and enables them to have a pleasant game. A course that is too difficult means continued trouble and frustration for them, and who can call that pleasure?

Power carts can be rented at most courses and these reduce the physical effort required. Choose the course that suits you. Husband and wife can play together. Another advantage of taking up golf is that it is available everywhere you go. It can be a real interest on a southern winter holiday. You can learn at any age. If you regard it as a pleasant outdoor experience, rather than a challenge to become an expert, you can learn to play well enough. Courses are not crowded in the off hours during weekdays and you will be welcome as a learner at that time. Join a club or "pay as you play." It need not be expensive.

(b) Lawn Bowling

This game has been a favourite for centuries and has stood the test of time. One of the early historical matches played nearly four hundred years ago, was the famous one in which Sir Francis Drake was engaged when the excited messenger announced that the feared Spanish Armada had been sighted and was coming to invade England. To stop it was entrusted to Sir Francis, but he was so immersed in the game that he did not rush off with usual cries of "To Horse!" He calmly stayed to finish his game. Perhaps he had a bet on and was leading. If he won the impending battle, he could use the earnings to celebrate and, if he lost . . . well, there was no unemployment insurance in those days and Elizabeth I was known to back winners exclusively.

The game has continued to be popular and is widely played on outdoor greens which are small level areas of carefully tended lawn.

They are usually well fenced and reserved for the sport. This is important, for a rough or bumpy surface can deflect the shot. It is surprising what can happen to the green if it is not fenced and locked. Some years ago, one September afternoon, those relaxing in the bar at the Banff Springs Hotel were treated to the sight of two mature bull elks chasing each other around. Perhaps they were just looking for a suitable site to settle who was the better but, in any event, they squared off on the bowling green just outside the door. After several loud bugles, they lowered their heads, charged, clashed, dug in their hooves and pushed. The turf flew and the green was plowed. Now the barkeeper had sampled his wares and was full of induced courage, so he promptly rushed out to chase the intruders. A swift kick to one drew their attention, at which they promptly wheeled in unison, lowered their heads and charged. The barkeeper, now full of wisdom, rushed the door. Fortunately it was the small one ushed as an exit, so the large hatracks on the elks prevented pursuit. Confused, they ambled off to think it over, and the remainder of the green was saved.

In many respects, lawn bowling is like curling though less strenuous. Two teams compete against each other and men and ladies both participate. It is a fine summer outdoor activity and you will be welcome. There is a local club in

(c) Fishing

Summer, with its better weather and open water is the usual season for fishing but ice fishing has become very popular now that improved facilities are available. Snowmobiles and tracked vehicles have made safe transportation to more distant spots a routine operation. You need not have your own vehicle as transportation is often provided to the rental fish huts.

However, summer is, of course, still the most popular time for this sport. Fishing has always fascinated both men and women. Now that you have the time, you will be surprised to find how many places there are for reasonable fishing, even in or near very crowded cities! Spend some time around the available water, ask questions at the marinas, tackle stores, etc. and you may be pleasantly surprised. Rental tackle, directions and advice are obtainable at such places. Start in this manner if you are inexperienced and you will know better what to buy if you decide to continue with the sport.

(d) Boating

Boating is available on almost any water. If you don't own a boat, start off by renting and take it from there as your interest develops. It is best to have some experienced person accompany you in the beginning as there are many possible hazards with which the uninitiated are not familiar.

(e) Walking and Hiking

Don't neglect walking as a combined form of sport, or physical activity, and an interesting way to enjoy time. It is an activity which your doctor will probably recommend but, usually to be of value, it should be done at a suitable pace and for a long enough distance. One soon becomes tired of walking the same beats with the same sights, so why not introduce variety? Try new sections in either the city or country. Most people who have lived in an area have not seen its points of interest, the ones that the sightseeing tours visit. Why not plan your walks to cover your accessible districts of possible interest? You may be surprised at what has been there all these years and fascinated with the new developments going up today. Clubs and similar organizations often plan "walks" to interest people in activities such as wildlife, the preservation of an area as parkland, or bird watching. These are advertised and the public invited. Why not go at least once to see if you enjoy it?

Non-Seasonal Activities

(a) Politics

Everyone should be interested in politics and government. That is the basis of democracy. Federal and provincial members have "riding" associations which remain active between elections. Most locally-elected persons and members of their opposition also have some organization. Much of the work is done by volunteers. Choose a candidate, or something you wish to support and turn up at the meeting. Join the organization. Offer to help. You will be welcome; this is just what is needed and can develop into a real interest for you. At election time, there is often paid work within the association or at polling booths. Such jobs, of course, go to the faithful who were there ahead of time. Don't ignore this activity if you have an interest in the government at any of the three levels.

It will also help to keep the views and needs of retired persons before the politicians.

Hobbies with Possible In-depth Involvement

There are many hobbies which can become of absorbing interest and which are continually expanding in skill, knowledge and technology. Involvement in one of these can lead to a desire to progress to the more advanced steps and steadily improve in its execution. Some, such as the following, have almost unending possibilities and are usually accompanied by membership of a very active club or group which provides opportunities for an expanding circle of friends and social activities.

(a) Gardening

One such hobby is gardening. It is generally thought of as simply planting a garden with seeds or boxed plants, watering it, weeding it and watching it grow. But this is only the beginning. If your interest develops, you can read up on those plants in which you have an interest and become an expert. You may then go on to plant breeding and even the development of new strains. The hobby opens the way to flower shows, clubs and the making of friends with like interests. Growing need not stop with the summer. Indoor gardening under lights, often of a sophisticated nature, is very common. A greenhouse can be relatively inexpensive, but is not necessary. Fluorescent lights now permit the establishment of a garden in the basement at practically no cost! You may grow winter blooms or have your plants started indoors and ready to transplant when spring arrives. Apartment balcony gardens are common in season and, in locations where vegetable garden plots can be rented, these are becoming popular with the higher food prices.

(b) Photography

Photography has a very wide range of possibilities. Everyone enjoys looking at pictures. But a good one requires skill as well as luck and involves composition, lighting, timing, etc. Each can be studied to decide how it could be improved. Then there is the possibility of developing your own negatives, printing, enlarging and going into colour. This hobby can be pursued with an inexpensive camera or can be expanded as far as your interest desires and your finances permit. Camera clubs are everywhere. Their members will welcome you and are most willing to teach and advise new members.

(c) Bird Watching

In addition to just bird watching (finding and observing birds), studying identifying marks, recording normal seasonal migration for each and looking for unusual species are fascinating. Records will indicate when to expect migratory movements which may be anticipated and observed. Local clubs often gather annual records. Public participation is invited in such efforts. You may contribute worthwhile information. Such interest again leads to group membership, activities and new friends. A bird feeder in your garden can keep you busy observing.

Production Hobbies

There are many other hobbies, some of which can be classified as straight production and which satisfy the needs of many people. Carpentry is an example. Make furniture, boats, cupboards, panel a wall, put on additions or build a sleeping cabin at the cottage. Some people enjoy making up models from kits, others from plans, many of great complexity requiring considerable skill in workmanship. If you have not had some experience and need training, technical schools or community colleges or the "Y" often provide courses. There is probably someone in your senior citizens' group who would be happy to teach you the basics. Once you learn how to measure, cut, join, smooth and nail properly, you have the rudiments to do almost anything. Your early efforts may be rough but, with practice and a serious interest, you can become quite proficient. The library has many books showing the structural methods used in making anything from a doghouse to a violin and specifying the kind of wood to be used. One man glowed with pride as he told of his hobby of making pictures from pieces of different coloured wood, carefully cut out to fit together. These were then attached to a firm backing. Remember, good ones are often saleable too.

Creative Activities

(a) Painting

Some people are creative by nature and must use this gift to feel fulfilled. One of the most common ways of doing this is by painting. If you have such an interest, there are groups of people available almost everywhere who help each other and may employ an instructor. Many school boards have night school. It could lead on to more serious study involving private lessons. Once you become involved in art, you discover a whole new world. You see things so much more clearly and appreciate the real beauty. An art gallery takes on a new interest and a quick trip through one is no longer enough. You can spend a day studying one painting! Local exhibitions become an event to watch for.

If you are creative, try different things until you find the application which interests you. It may be clay modelling, carving or whatever, but such an interest becomes fascinating and engrossing once you get into it. Don't neglect such a talent if you have one. It doesn't matter what it is as long as you enjoy it. You will probably find joining a group and obtaining instruction most important.

Libraries and Reading

You may find hobbies which have no cost. An example of this is the public library. It is full of all kinds of books; just interesting reading, instructive titles, current magazines, etc. Generally, you can go and read them there or take them home. Many very interesting hours may be spent in this manner even if you only look at the pictures! It is an interest which can be enjoyed when desired -- and you should have as many of these as possible to fill in otherwise blank days. If you walk into a library with no object in mind and simply look around, read titles and thumb through pictorials, you will almost certainly find yourself taking down one or more books or magazines and becoming interested.

It will be surprising if it doesn't result in your taking books home and starting to read much more. It may also awaken an interest in some hobby about which you choose to read and which might not otherwise have occurred to you. If you don't use a library regularly, some day when there is nothing else before you, visit one and let nature take its course!

Continuing Education

If you have thought of continuing your education, now is the time. In recent years there has been a very great broadening in the opportunities to do so, in the range of programmes offered and in entrance requirements. There are basically two classifications. The first is the study of more serious disciplines, often with the idea of attaining a standing or degree. If you wish to attain high school or university graduation status, you can often do this through a local institution. Now more than ever such instruction may be obtained by mail. University degrees, in particular, have become much more readily available in this way. Some provide, in addition to written material, tape recordings and the right to phone your professor long distance, at no cost to you! Entrance requirements have also been reduced for the "mature student."

As an example of the attitude of many universities, the Sir Wilfred Laurier in Waterloo, Ontario, is offering students of over sixty-five years of age the opportunity of taking the regular daytime or evening courses with the full-time students, at no cost! One may take two such courses per year on this basis. It was stated that this was done because of the growing desire to provide stimulating interests for senior citizens. Many other universities are now offering some similar programme. Since the above announcement was made, the University of Toronto, Department of Extension, has announced somewhat similar opportunities. If you wish to participate, contact personally or write to the appropriate institutions in your province.

The second classification includes those subjects which lead to the development of skills which may be saleable or simply for interest. There is a very rapidly broadening range of institutions teaching many of these things. They include art, house repairs, gourmet cooking and acting, in the hobby field. They also teach a wide range of commercial subjects. If you want part-time employment, you may find that a course will either provide new skills for you or bring rusty ones up to saleable standards. You may be able to take such a course in the evening to be ready for retirement, or it may be best for you to take it as a full-time activity after you have stopped working.

Hobbies

Hobbies can have the dual purpose of providing an enjoyable activity plus income from the sale of your product. To be saleable, it must meet acceptable commercial standards, which means professional standards. How to obtain this training is perhaps dependent on the hobby and your location. Most boards of education, community colleges and technical schools have inexpensive classes that may fill your needs. Private lessons will cost more but may be the final requirement to develop a really professional finish. In some instances, there are privately-run trade schools which aim to develop a commercial standard of skill in a trade in which employment is available.

It is often a distinct advantage to strive for saleable results from your hobby. It provides a goal and forces you to try to improve, practice and keep at it. This will assist in overcoming the lethargy and loss of interest which can so easily come to the retired person who no longer is subject to the demands and discipline of a job. Selling your work can also give that sense of achievement and success that may otherwise be lacking. Continued training may be the means of achieving the desirable standard and sustaining your interest.

Social Activities

On the job, most of your time was probably spent with people. This became part of your life, filled a need and was an extra important bonus. Many fellow employees became friends. Often social activities, bowling leagues, etc. were centred here. Even those persons whose company you did not like were part of your daily contact with people. Most of us are gregarious and need regular contact with a number of persons. Retirement is the end of the job connection. Once you retire, all those contacts cease and it is you and your spouse alone at home, unless you go out and find opportunities to be with people. While working you may not have needed these, but now it is different. Retirement often brings deep loneliness. Fortunately, the others in the same position will feel likewise and there will be plenty of opportunities to find the companionship you require.

Our old reliable senior citizens' groups is specifically designed for this purpose, so that is your first stop. From there on, other associations should be made with a view to specific interests. It may be a bridge club, a fraternal society or some group that comes together to further a hobby or because of a common interest. Such associations will fill a real requirement in your life.

Entertainment

Entertainment has a new place now. You have much more time and you can spend it in this very enjoyable way. You are free to choose the most suitable time when the entertainment is most readily available and the prices are lowest. In addition, very many organizations have special discounts or prices for senior citizens. Sometimes these are restricted to certain times and will not apply to the normally busy periods. But you get much more for your entertainment dollar. Some theatre chains issue special identifying cards which you must show to purchase the ticket at a discount. Enquire from your friends and at the local theatres which you might attend to determine their method of handling the discount. They will tell you what proof of age is required and issue your identification application. It is often possible to do even better, for organizations form groups to attend at such times and may get further group discounts. A chartered bus, if required, may reduce the transportation cost and add to the fun. Look into the opportunities which are available. Read the advertisements and, above all, ask your other retired friends. Most of them take great pride in being a source of information and are very pleased to be asked for it. Don't hesitate to enquire if there are special senior citizens' rates. Many places have, but often don't publish them.

Travel

The points made in the section on entertainment respecting special rates, times and group transportation apply equally well to travel. Off-season and group plans are often surprisingly low. If you have a desire to travel, either for

sightseeing purposes or just to go somewhere different during certain periods of the year, look into it. Take the time
to do so fully. That time is available now. Enquire about the
conducted "package" tour groups. Wherever you go -- to the
local museum, Florida or St. Peter's in Rome, for a trip up
the Nile, or to see the Great Buddha in Japan -- you will
see them. They have many advantages, more so now that
you are older and can use the extra help. The tour cost is
usually fixed. The conductor looks after all baggage, hotels,
transportation and, perhaps, meals. If not, he can advise
the best places to go, what to avoid and how to conform to
local customs. The inevitable problems are his. You are
free of the local "gyp" artists. You will probably find compatible companions in the group and will have someone responsible if you need assistance. You are free to go off on
your own to make those local contacts you hear about and,
if you have a connection which makes this possible, by all
means do so! On balance, these advantages, plus the substantial saving in cost, make the "package" tour the logical
choice for retired people. Even singles find travelling to
very distant places quite satisfactory with such a group.
Ask air, bus and rail lines about fares, package plans, etc.
Travel agents often have specials. Look around. It is surprising what is available. Don't give up because you think
the expense will be too great. At least investigate before
doing so. There are many low-cost package tours, charter
flights, group plans, etc. You may be pleasantly surprised
by what you can afford.

Volunteer Work

Shakespeare once said, in the "Merchant of Venice":
"Mercy . . . is twice blest, it blesseth him that gives and
him that takes." The same can be said of volunteer work.
There are two sides to it and both offer benefits. There is
a tremendous need for persons willing to give assistance
to disadvantaged persons like the aged, the lame, the sick,
the blind and those too poorly endowed by nature to ade-
quately compete for a decent standard of living in this world.
Most persons who lead normal lives have little or no contact
with them. They are hidden away and are not seen. Their
need is so great that there is not enough money nor are there
enough willing helpers to do all that is needed.

If you have time to give and a desire to help, there is plenty of scope for you. It would be impossible to list all the things that are done by volunteers (those who work without pay), but the range is broad. There are various activities at the Red Cross such as driving and assisting at blood donor clinics. Help the blind by reading to them, writing their letters or just visiting. Assist with crippled children. Answer the phone at Distress Centres. Deliver "meals on wheels" to shut-ins and lonely persons. There are also many church-sponsored jobs. For the executive, there is work at board level, in the financial campaign, and, often, with all the planning and organizing to start a new activity.

In this work, the helped person frequently benefits greatly and there can be much satisfaction derived by the person giving the assistance.

However, the personality of the individual volunteer must be taken into account when he or she is selecting an activity of this type. Many cannot work with or face those with certain disabilities or who live in difficult situations. But the choice of activities is so broad that anyone should be able to find a suitable one. If you don't know of a starting place, ask any religious leader for suggestions. Try the "Y", the Community Chest office or the Red Cross. Many cities have a volunteer centre to advise those wishing to do volunteer work of available opportunities. Someone will take an interest, so enquire and locate a function suitable for you.

CHAPTER 10

FOR YOUR HAPPINESS AND PEACE OF MIND

The phrases "retirement shock," "armchair suicide" and others like them arose because of the very real reaction of many persons to retirement. Fortunately, because the reasons are real, they can be identified and surmounted. Money worries and the problem of how to spend one's time have already been considered.

But there are still others. To understand them properly, it is best to review the period through which the persons retired or approaching retirement have come and to see how the major events of this period have formed the opinions by which they live. The world was so different when they entered it as a young person starting out in life. There was very little security, the "work ethic" was unquestioned, and pensions and retirement were not expected. There was no thinking which prepared these people for voluntary retirement before physical disability forced it, and it was sprung on them too late in their lives to permit ready and unquestioned acceptance of the principle in their subconscious mind. As a result, they expected to work until old age forced a stop, well past sixty-five. They feel guilty if they do not continue to do so. It is difficult for them to believe that the pension cheques will continue without that work. They have heard that many of the retired are having a difficult time and do not know if they too will suffer the same fate. Not having been mentally prepared for it, many feel that retirement is a direct statement that they are too old to be of further use, not just in the job but in anything. They believe they no longer have a valid reason to continue.

These thoughts are understandable but it is obvious that they are out-of-date and no longer apply.

The sudden shock caused by the abrupt overnight termination of your job, coupled with the necessity of finding a completely new use for most of your waking time, is a real and serious problem. It gives rise to many thoughts of which you were never previously aware. These are all in your mind. The physical is a much easier adjustment. Problems of the mind do not go away simply by asking them to do so or by having someone tell you they are groundless. The solution lies in understanding why they have arisen and in eliminating their causes. Once this is done, those fears will evaporate and the resulting vaccuum can be filled with confidence and a zest for your new life.

Look back over the period through which you have lived and think about how it has formed your opinions. You will see that those reasons, while factual at the time, no longer hold true and that there is every justification for putting them out of your mind and replacing them with the facts as they exist today.

Those attaining their sixty-fifth birthday in 1975 were born in 1910. They became sixteen in 1926. If their employment commenced in that year, they entered a very different world from that in which we live today. There was no unemployment insurance. There were no state-sponsored medical or hospital plans. Industrial pensions were almost non-existent and only a very rare person expected to eventually have one. Everyone knew that he must work to live. Then came the traumatic experience of the Great Depression with its serious financial hardships which left most persons who were of working age with scars and fears which remain with them. Financial insecurity was to be feared and work was the defence against it. Those retiring now and within the next few years belong to this group and their thinking will be conditioned by that background.

It is a very important factor in their psychological reaction to retirement. They grew up with the motor car, the airplane and the radio, and the electronic wonders are simply the kind of development they take for granted in scientific matters. But to stop working at, perhaps, sixty-five and to be able to continue living in substantially the same life style is a concept which first appeared to them during their fifties. It is difficult, at least in their subconscious minds, to accept this as real and to relax with it as an earned right.

Those born twenty years later will have a different outlook and the 1950 babies will have come into such a new era that there will be no similarity with the earlier groups in most of these aspects. No wonder there is a generation gap.

Many of those who retired a few years ago are having a difficult time and the knowledge of their experience frightens those facing retirement now. This is why it is so important to understand that their situation is much different than it is for those retiring today.

Those retiring in 1965 or before had no Canada Pension and any industrial pension would be very small by today's standard. Any such pensions that did exist would not likely have had an escalation clause. So these persons will often be living on the Old Age Security Pension and Supplement plus whatever private means they possessed. Those who sold their homes then received much less for them than they would today and, if they invested that money in non-cashable long-term investments, the rate of interest was probably about one half of what it would be today. If the same persons retired now, their income would be, perhaps, three times as much, insofar as it is derived from government pensions and income from the sale of a home.

Those who are retiring now or who have already done so must live with the facts with which they have arrived at retirement age. Pension consultants often state that, while hard figures are not available, they doubt that more than 1% of those retiring today have any significant industrial pension. This is why such pensions have been ignored in our calculations. Obviously, it was no better ten years ago.

In addition they have been most severely hit by the retired person's most dated enemy -- inflation. Everyone retiring fears and worries about it. However, now there is a difference. As we shall see in later chapters, inflation and its effects are generally recognized and much is being done to assist the retired person to cope with it today. Both the Canada and Old Age Security Pensions now have a built-in escalation factor which increases them after your retirement at the same rate as the cost of living increases. Obviously, this is a most important help in eliminating the fear of inflation.

97

There seems to be some question whether or not this escalation or index does really increase as fast as the cost of living. This is perhaps because one day the rent goes up 15% (it won't change again till the lease is up) or meat increases twenty cents per pound, and the pension cheques received that day are just the same as those cashed thirty days ago. This may be true, but the escalation index for the Canada Pension is calculated on the change over a twelve-month period. The Old Age Security Pension is re-calculated and revised every three months. Each January the Canada Pension payments are changed. If the cost of living has gone up 10% in the last year, it will go up 10%. The Old Age Pension is calculated on the shorter period and the jumps will be smaller, but will come each quarter and will be increased at the same rate as the cost of living index. At the end of a year it too should reflect the same cost of living rise and be up by the same percentage.*

We have seen why those persons retiring from insurable employment today are much better off than their older brothers and sisters who retired earlier. Many of the stories that one hears about their financial problems are inaccurate, incomplete or are the result of circumstances that may not pertain to you. Ignore them. Fall back on the basic approach that your retirement life is yours personally. The experience of others may not be parallel. Make your own financial determination and life plan. This will provide you with firm and convincing answers which will at one stroke wipe out those fears and replace them with satisfactory answers applying specifically to you. This will be convincing. It seems to be a human trait to exaggerate things and to enjoy telling stories of hardships borne either by the raconteur

---

*Monthly amount of Old Age Security Pension payments at dates shown.

1973:   July to September -- $100.00
           October to December -- $105.30
1974:   January to March -- $108.14
           April to June -- $110.09
           July to September -- $112.95
           October to December -- $117.02

or others. Inaccurate information is most common and the public media are frequently guilty of this. Much of the publicity respecting retirement sets out to emphasize the difficulties and concentrate on the exception rather than the norm.

As an example, there was a recent newspaper article reported to be the statements of a person who will retire in 1975 at the age of sixty-five. He had calculated his post-retirement living expenses and was concerned that his industrial pension, combined with the Canada Pension, would fall a little short of meeting these expenses. The actual figures were shown and this was so. However, no mention was made of the Old Age Security Pension for which the indicated length of Canadian employment would certainly qualify him. When this was added in he would have a very comfortable surplus! Soon his wife would draw hers too, making the surplus just that much greater.

It is for these reasons that so much care was taken in previous chapters to look into the financial picture and help you to decide how to build an income and expenditure balance that will put your mind at ease and enable you to develop your life plan along the lines which you desire. It may require some compromises but so have all other periods of your life. These financial arrangements and spending patterns on which you have decided are not necessarily fixed for life. You have the right to make adjustments as you go along. Perhaps there will be opportunities to increase income. Perhaps there will be changes in the way in which you spend it. Do as you wish, but be accurate and know the facts to stay out of financial difficulties.

The use of your time is of equal importance. Most persons must occupy themselves and their minds with activities which satisfy their personal needs. These, of course, vary broadly with the individual. This is why it has been constantly emphasized that **you** must make the choices. No one else can. Know your true inner feelings and make the proper selection for **you**.

Do not misunderstand. Selfishness is a narrow way leading to loneliness and unhappiness. What is referred to here is a contrast, to emphasize the difference between two periods of your life. In the years when you were raising the family, your personal wishes were often sacrificed to enable the family to have theirs. Frequently, you stayed with an unpleasant job just to keep the pay cheque coming. Now the family has been taken care of and pension and investment cheques come in without further work. The desires of you and your spouse are paramount and you are free to indulge them. It is no longer a case of putting your wishes ahead of those for whom you are responsible.

The selfishness referred to here then is the selection of activities of your choice, for which you are mentally and physically endowed and which you require for personal fulfillment. In these activities, the need for friends and group activities and the desire to help others has been constantly emphasized, but do these things in a manner suitable to you. Trying to ape another person with a different mind could be a catastrophe.

A direct search for happiness will fail; it is a by-product of a satisfying life, a mental state induced by peace of mind and the satisfaction of those needs and desires both for yourself and toward others, which your personality requires.

It is often thought that achieving one's goal or possessing certain things will bring happiness, but this is not true. It is the elimination of thoughts which bother you that makes room for and admits happiness. While it is true this may mean the possession of more adequate housing or some other physical item, if its attainment still leaves thoughts which disturb your peace of mind, happiness cannot be there. It is an attitude, the feeling that you are discharging your responsibilities and are doing the things with your life that you want to do.

When the great range of possible activities discussed earlier is considered, it is obvious that no one can really say that there is nothing to do. If a person says that nothing takes the place of work and that he or she cannot adjust to life without it, then let that person work as a volunteer! However, it may just be one manifestation of the shock of this very important change. And to fear the change is a normal reaction. But, by understanding what has occurred in life and what can be done about it, we have seen that one can come out with an arm full of roses or smelling of violets, if you prefer.

Some persons simply give in, watch TV, drink and decline, awaiting the end. Surely, after our investigation of this subject in the previous chapter, you will plan something much better than that. You have worked all your life for this opportunity, now seize it and make it one of the happy periods of your life.

But it is up to you! You must get up, get out, make contacts, select your interest and participate. If asked to select the most important thing for a retired person to do, the choice here would be to get out to some place where he or she would contact other retired persons and try to find common interests. Anyone working in this field can quote endless examples of problems which arose when a person simply stayed at home and of how these problems were solved when that person got out and became involved in things of interest. It is preferable to be fatigued from over-work than bored and frustrated from inactivity.

Most people experience a feeling of guilt when they stop working. You were taught to believe that work was good in itself, and to not work was "lazy," "bad" or "no good." Now you are not working and your mind automatically turns up those unpleasant names. Your defence against this is the knowledge that those names no longer apply to you. You have reached the age of retirement, have done your part, earned your leisure, and are not expected to continue.

You may have thought the term "senior citizens" simply an insincere attempt to soothe the feelings of those too old to work. However, to use a slang phrase, those who govern and still work have "put their money where their mouth is." You can't call the universal Old Age Security Pension and all the other state-paid assistance plans insincere. They pay off in hard cash, not words. There are also those many helpful benefits, such as reduced fares. All these add up to a sincere and concrete, "Thank you, you have done your job. Now we will do the work and share its output with you for the rest of your life." What more can you ask to free your mind from this feeling of guilt?

Another common reaction is, "It's all over now, there is nothing more I can accomplish, why carry on?" If that were true, it might be valid. But the truth is that there is a great deal you can do other than at your old job. There is still a need for your efforts. These may be socially more valuable! Everyone knows of course you can't work as hard as you did when you were younger but, if you feel the need to make a contribution, select the area of your choice and go to it.

If one looks into the matter, it soon becomes apparent that there is a great need for further help of all kinds amongst the "disadvantaged" persons. All the help needed is not available if the money was there to pay for it. If you undertake some of this work on a volunteer basis, you are doing work that would be paid for if the money was available. We value work by the price paid for it, but a greater recognition of the value of this unpaid work is growing and being publicly acknowledged. Perhaps it should be valued by the results achieved. You are needed. There is such a range of jobs waiting that everyone can find one to do.

Nothing could be better than to select an interest which would assist not only in preserving the heritage given to you but building upon and increasing it before passing it on to succeeding generations. This can be done in many ways. No one man is expected to make a monumental change in things but each tree planted, each person helped or each organization assisted is a contribution in that direction.

If you have a family, and perhaps grandchildren, there is lots of scope for assisting here. A family is a group of related persons who, since the human race began, have helped each other. It is one of our strongest built-in drives. You have always achieved satisfaction from unselfish assistance to your family and will continue to do so. Your contribution, now in terms of personal assistance rather than financial, is still needed and will be appreciated.

Are you not morally obligated to help your spouse enjoy these years? Your attitude and assistance in this respect now is of more importance than anything anyone else can do.

At a wedding reception, the master of ceremonies said, "Without a sense of achievement, there can be no happiness, or significance to long life." Set your sights on goals that are appropriate for you at this stage and then work to achieve them and enjoy the happiness that will come from doing so.

In conclusion, first you must accept your new position as a person who has earned retirement and who, therefore, is no longer subject to the claims of pre-retirement days. Then you must build a personally satisfying retirement life.

If you have been successful in these matters, you will be able to look back at a later date and know that your time was well used. Perhaps you assisted your spouse, family or those who were less fortunate when assistance was needed. Perhaps you have added to the heritage which you received. If you can claim some of these, then surely you will have found peace of mind and happiness during retirement. If so, your third problem area has also been solved.

CHAPTER 11

INFLATION AND THE RETIRED

The Problem -- Assistance and Defence

Inflation has become one of the major and steadily growing concerns of the retired. There is good reason for this and, to the extent that the cost of living rises in any period and your income does not increase, the ability to purchase your needs is reduced. So, for the retired, who in the past frequently had fixed incomes, this can be a worry. Now we shall see a very important measure of relief that has been introduced into the picture.

While the rate of inflation varies from year to year, it appears to be continuing upward and the hopes widely held a few years ago that it would start to decline seem unreal today. It should be made clear here that this is not to be construed as a forecast for the future. There is no agreement, even amongst respected economists, on what the future course will be. They have been very wrong in many recent forecasts and may be so again.

The following is a review of the past to show how to protect yourselves should inflation continue. If it does, what must the retired person prepare to face?

You should remember that this is not a new problem. It has been a continuous worldwide one, probably since the use of value exchange and money came into being thousands of years ago.

History is full of instances of the debasement of the coinage, shortages, famine, etc. which all lead to inflation. Sometimes it was on a temporary basis till the next good harvest, sometimes the results were more permanent. Other than during short periods of depression, inflation has continued at a varying pace with pronounced outbursts from time to time in response to some special cause. Always, it has burnt itself out and the more moderate rate has resumed.

Rulers and governments have tended to create money for selfish, or other, reasons which as a side effect increased prices. When the Spanish acquired the large gold and silver accumulations from the Indian peoples in Central and South America, the result was inflation. And, insofar as can be ascertained, wars have always been accompanied by it.

"The Hedge"

Inflation has been so steadily prevalent in Europe and the East for so long that their peoples have learned to mistrust paper money or fixed value securities and favour the ownership of tangible things. These include land, buildings, precious metals, gems and objects of art, which are considered a hedge against it. Such a hedge can be anything that is in limited supply, has a production and distribution cost, is in demand by people and for which the value will hopefully increase along with the general price level. Thus, at any time it can be sold for cash and its increase in value will provide the extra money to purchase as much of other commodities at the higher price as could have been bought with the cash at the time when the hedge was purchased. If one simply held back during the period of price rise, that cash would purchase less at the end than at the beginning of the period. The hedge, by increasing in value as inflation progresses, is designed to prevent this.

An obvious example at the time of writing is gold. Its supply is limited and production cannot be increased rapidly. The demand for it has increased and its price, while fluctuating, has risen steadily so that, over a period of a few recent years, it has gone up four times in value! Someone with $1,000 cash a few years ago could have bought twenty-five ounces of gold and could sell it for about $3,500 today (summer of 1974). If the same person had decided to simply hold on to his $1,000 cash, at the termination of the period his money could buy less because of the increase in the general price level. Obviously this hedge would have protected him from the effects of inflation. Most hedges do not perform so dramatically or successfully. Such speculation is too sophisticated for any but a few to undertake. What can the rest do?

It is not the purpose of this book to advise specifically respecting particular investments, but the retention of those assets that you already own and that are of lasting value, such as property, art, antiques, furniture, jewellery and collections, should be considered. Many readers will also be qualified to go further in specific fields in which they are more knowledgeable. Others will take the time to investigate and learn more about such matters in order to help themselves.

It is clear that the retired people must be very wary of gambling lest they lose and must carefully preserve what they have. A young working person has time to recoup losses, even if just through years of working, but the retired person no longer enjoys that position. So "**caution** is the **watchword**."

Government Acceptance of the Responsibility

Because inflation is such an old and well-known problem, we can learn from the past. Such a study may show the way. But now a new dimension has been added. It is the birth of a new, humane understanding of the problem, coupled with positive action to help.

Our governments on all three levels have recognized the seriousness of inflation and are helping in a constructive way. This is a new and most important development. Their actions and words indicate that they accept the responsibility of enabling the retired to cope with inflation. It cannot be over-emphasized that this is brand new in the world, so far as we know, and it is difficult to think of any step of greater financial importance to the retired. The list of new programmes of assistance is expanding and additions to the existing ones keep appearing. It is impressive.

In effect, these governments are providing a hedge against inflation, at least insofar as the income which they provide is concerned. Such provisions, making payments flexible in relationship to a known index such as the cost of living is now called "indexing" and is a term you will hear more frequently and should understand.

Escalation in Pension Cheques

The Old Age Security Pension now has an escalation clause. It is reviewed quarterly and will be raised each quarter if circumstances warrant. In 1970, it was $79.85 per month. Then, in 1973, the policy of regular quarterly increases was established and, by October 1974, it was $117.02. That means there was almost a 50% increase in four years against a cost of living index of over 30%! Current increases in the Old Age Security and Canada Pension now are adjusted regularly to parallel the rise in the cost of living.

When discussing the pension during our examination of expected retirement income, we noted the increasing importance of the Canada Pension. In the ten-year period from 1966-75, this may well have doubled a working person's expected income from the combined Old Age Security and Canada Pension.

At this point it is not necessary to go into the mechanics by which the Canada Pension is calculated, but let is suffice to say that the starting pension is now increasing much more rapidly and will continue to do so because of the cumulative effect of the recent large increases in the "maximum pensionable earnings," brought about in 1973 and 1974. When the plan was introduced in 1966, the maximum annual pension planned for those retiring on January 1, 1975 was $1,250 but the escalation provisions have already increased this to an estimated $1,440 and it will probably be increased to a maximum starting rate of over $1,600 on January 1, 1976. Most of this increase is recent and, by law, will continue if necessitated by inflation.

The important thing is that the retired person who draws a Canada Pension will have his pension increased annually. This is done to a set formula. The percentage increase in the cost of living from November to October over the similar period twelve months earlier is added to the pension cheques for the next year, starting in January.

Realize what this means. In the past, those on "fixed incomes" **were** on fixed incomes. Once a pension was set, it didn't change. Prices might rise but income did not. This was the real problem. Now the situation, so far as these government-sponsored pensions are concerned, has completely changed. These pensions need no longer be classed as fixed income.

They now cover the basic costs of the necessities of an average couple. In the list of living expenses of the retired couple in Chapter 6, page 45, their annual costs were as follows.

House	$1,301
Food	1,250
Utilities	250
Clothing	450
Personal care	100
Medical and health	175
Total	$3,526

All of these items are included in the cost-of-living index and any increases should, therefore, be reflected in it. If both partners qualify for the Old Age Security Pension and one partner for the maximum Canada Pension, starting January 1, 1975, the two in combination will probably draw a total in excess of $4,300 plus any increases added by indexing in the period. This is greater than the cost of these necessities. The couple will be protected then, in that any increase in their basic cost of living will be equalled by increases in their pensions.

If you have enjoyed a more expensive standard of living which is above these pension totals, it would perhaps be wise to develop a long-range plan to adjust your living costs and income to cope with the possible increases. The suggestions made in Chapter 7 will make a good starting point. These are expanded further in the last part of this chapter and the two together may provide the solution for you.

Government Payment of Certain Expenses

The next item of great importance to the retired community is the government-sponsored medical and hospital plans. Once, serious illness could lead to crippling expenses often resulting in a crippling financial situation. Now this has all changed. Medical care costs have gone up drastically, but the great financial fear they once held for the senior citizen has largely vanished with the provincial hospital and medical plans.

There is an increasing number of tax exemptions, some with built-in escalators. In 1973, the Federal exemption for all persons was increased and it was specifically stated that this was because of inflation. The extra exemption for those over sixty-five was increased, too. While such measures as changes in tax schedules and standard exemptions are part of the annual budget and are passed by Parliament in session, the new principle of increasing personal income tax exemption to help offset inflation has been adopted and is likely to continue. There is also a host of provisions available to retired persons for rebate of provincial and municipal taxes. Enquire about those which come under provincial and municipal jurisdiction in the province and municipality in which you reside. As an example, the province of Ontario has three programmes which are geared to help the senior citizens in 1974. Application is to be made when they submit their 1973 Federal income tax returns. Those persons who pay no tax will complete the Federal tax form as a means of application.

Let Them Know!

All the schemes described above were put into effect by politicians who guessed that these measures were wanted by the majority of voters and would be considered important enough to bring support for them at the most important election of all times to any politician presently in office -- the next one! They, therefore, want to know how you received them. These steps were big and many were "way out." If you have opinions respecting any measure, speak out. The best time is, of course, when it is in the formative stage. Most new measures are hinted at and discussed in public, at least in the "throne speech." Often this is done to test public reaction. Let your local member and the minister responsible for the measure know how you feel. If you are a member of a group or organization which could be legitimately classified as interested, encourage it to support and publicize the wishes of its members. Politicians are more concerned about the opinions of organizations which represent a group than with those of an individual. However, when many individuals register their opinions, the politicians soon have a clear picture of what the majority thinks and how strongly they hold those views.

The percentage of retired people in the population is increasing rapidly, due both to the increase in the life span and the increasing number of persons being retired at a specific age. The weight of the opinions of this group is now felt. Realize that action can be important in bringing about desired legislation. Do your part! Write or phone your members, both Federal and provincial, or drop in to see them if they have a local office.

Your Part in Handling Inflation

The measures discussed above were made for you, not by you. As an individual you could neither initiate nor stop them.

However, there is still that part of your income and assets that is under your own control and which you must handle yourself. This will now be considered.

(a) Fixed Contract Investments -- Bonds, Mortgages, Etc.

The obvious aim in investment is to have the income increase at the same rate as or better than the price level or the rate of inflation. If inflation ceases, no income increase is necessary. A little elementary thought on the matter soon brings a realization that a fixed contract on which the income is set for its term cannot accomplish this aim.

(b) Common Stocks

It has been the hope of many that the ownership of common stocks might be the solution. In many cases it has done so where the corporation has been able to increase its dividends from time to time at a satisfactory rate. However, this is not a sure bet. The dividends of many corporations have remained unchanged or have been reduced or eliminated. Many "stocks" have declined over the last few years. This route is for the experienced.

Most investment advisors would suggest that you avoid having too much of your money invested in speculative securities and that you confine speculation to that portion of money you can afford to risk and lose without serious consequences. Seek good advice and use your own judgment. Another factor to take into account is your reaction to risk. Some accept and live with it readily, others worry and fret with every move up or down. This can be an important point in your decision.

(c) Real Estate

The boom in prices of real estate in recent years has brought it into focus as perhaps one of the best investments and hedges against inflation. Whether it will continue to be so is, of course, anybody's guess. Almost anyone with a house, land, building, etc. has found it increasing in both selling price and rental value. Obviously, if one can retain the ownership and rent the property, providing that the rental can be increased with inflation, the income from it may be the hedge you seek. It is an interesting prospect and one which you should take into account when you are considering any change with respect to property you own. If you sell it, what will you do with the money? If you wish to leave your home because it is no longer suitable for your retirement life and you plan to go into a rental unit, why not consider renting out the house rather than selling it? Duplexing the house and renting one apartment has also been suggested. And, remember that, if you rent the property, there will be new factors affecting income taxes. Depreciation on the rented part will increase current exemption so full taxes perhaps need not be paid on the rental income. Find out about these matters if you contemplate renting. If you are not familiar with them, seek out the advice of a qualified accountant or lawyer to explain and calculate them for you. Take careful thought before you dispose of any property you own.

If you have undeveloped real estate and want to turn it into an income-producing asset, consider the possibility of leasing it, on a basis that includes an escalation clause or an increase in the annual rental under stipulated circumstances. Much property is now leased for commercial and industrial purposes with provisions of this nature. If you have property, perhaps it would be wise to consider the possibility of leasing it on such a basis rather than selling it outright.

Investing in property may be as good a hedge as keeping what you already own. Therefore, have this in mind if you have funds to invest. Purchasing property is not a simple undertaking. Those who are experienced in the field study it, learn about it and move only after they feel secure in doing what they plan. Have a trusted advisor check out your arithmetic. Move carefully. If you miss one or more deals that you attempt to make, don't be too disappointed! It is the best experience you can have and will enable you to confirm and clarify your thinking.

(d) Art, Jewels, Antiques, Coins, Stamps, Etc.

Many knowledgeable persons and corporations consider items in this category as one of the finest hedges. These do not produce an income and gain would only be realized through their eventual sale at a profit. You may have some such items which have become much more valuable than you realize, so do not dispose of anything which might fall within this classification without ascertaining its value from a reliable valuator.

If you have such property, what do you do? It's a personal decision which you make, placing the need for current cash against the possibility of getting a higher price later on when you might need it more. Perhaps you have collected these things as a hobby and would prefer to enjoy them as long as possible. At a later date, a specific need, a desire

113

for a trip, etc. might become the deciding factor in selling. If prices have risen substantially in the meantime, perhaps the price of your belongings will have gone up in proportion and the sale at that time will buy something which otherwise would have been too expensive.

A good example of this thinking has come to our attention. A husband and wife had both been interested in antiques for years and had built up a fine collection. It was largely in the form of furniture and ornaments with which they furnished the home. When the husband retired recently, a friend and antique dealer visited and offered to buy the house and contents, thus providing a substantial cash sum to augment the owners' pensions. The husband's answer was "no." The thinking behind it was that he had an adequate income at present and, if inflation continued, his things would probably increase in value too. If more cash was needed at any time, he could obtain it by selling these antiques piece by piece at the advanced prices. So now, in the meantime, the couple are enjoying living with them and taking satisfaction from the memories of their pleasure in finding, purchasing and often refinishing the pieces.

Start A Business?

Should you consider entering the business field now for a hobby, a part-time interest, a hedge? There is no reason why you should not, provided you have the means and knowledge to do so. To operate any business, of course, you must know what you are doing if you don't want to be burned. Often the best way is to buy an established business. It will be best if you study up and learn about it to be sure of your course. This in itself can be a very worthwhile undertaking, even if it never leads to more positive action. Many persons have built very rewarding and successful businesses after retirement. If you have the means, health, knowledge and desire to do so, it is your right to try.

Good luck!

CHAPTER 12

PUT YOUR AFFAIRS IN ORDER

Everyone has had the experience of looking for something that he or she is certain is around somewhere but can't find. Years later, it turns up in some unexpected place. This may have caused expense, an opportunity lost or trouble. He or she was the person who put it there and now can't remember having done so. Should anything happen to you, how will others find your necessary and valuable papers? There is a simple answer. Keep them all together in one secure and obvious place. Next, make a record of all those things which will be needed and advise several persons where this is kept. Make it a place where it can be easily found. What should it include?

1. Your birth certificate, required for insurance, etc.

2. Your Social Insurance number for pensions and many financial matters

3. Your marriage certificate (to certify the legal position of your spouse or children)

4. A list of any safety deposit boxes and their location, box and key numbers (not the same) and the location of the keys

5. All securities which you own and their location (It is generally advisable to have them registered.) Keep the purchase invoices, if they are available, and attach to the certificate to establish cost for capital gains or losses. If you do not have them, list cost prices and attach any supporting evidence which you may have such as cancelled cheques, records and correspondence.

6. The location of your will

7. All insurance (fire, life, etc.) and the location of policies

8. Details of property ownership, cost, mortgages, location of deed, tax bills, etc.

9. Leases, if any

10. Debts

11. Any legal paper of significance

12. A statement of any powers of attorney which you have granted

13. Burial plans, if you have made them

Power of Attorney

A "power of attorney" is of value should you become seriously ill or incapacitated and unable to act on your own behalf. If this occurs, those caring for you will be obliged either to do nothing with respect to transactions such as the sale of securities, which officially require your sanction, or to go through the cumbersome and expensive process of obtaining a court order to enable them to act for you. A properly-executed power of attorney gives someone the power to act on your behalf in such cases. Obviously, such authority should be granted only after very careful consideration and to a person or persons whom you can trust completely and in whose judgment you have confidence.

Why Have A Will?

A very important thing now for both partners is to have up-to-date wills. If you have one, it was perhaps written under different circumstances and was designed to accomplish other things than you wish today. Your disposble assets may have been, or will be, changed particularly if you sell your home. Those provisions made to take care of family responsibilities, if you had children at the time, may no longer be applicable. If this is the case, bring your will up to date.

If you don't have a will, you should put off making one no longer. Many persons have a great dislike for this act but, even if this is your feeling, don't let it stop you. It is an easy step, takes very little time, effort or expense and, when completed, can be filed away until needed or until changing circumstances require a revision. It is the only way in which you can direct that your wishes and responsibilities will be executed in the manner of your choice after you have gone.

The cost of a state-directed disposal of your property will be more expensive than under the normal procedure with a will. If there is no will, your assets are distributed according to law and this distribution may be very different from what you expect or wish it to be. The division under this arrangement can be a very complicated one, depending on the relationship of your surviving legal heirs. All this can be avoided and the distribution made according to your wishes by means of a will.

Your Will

What are the important factors to control through your will? It should dispose of your assets in the manner and to the persons you desire. It should be properly drawn to assume its acceptability to the courts and to avoid litigation. It should also take into account the way in which it attracts various death duties, keeping them at their minimum, and within the law, of course.

The requirements of a will are well established and a person can make his own. Self-Counsel Press has published "Wills and Probate Procedure" Guides for Ontario, B.C. and Alberta with a soon-to-be-published one for Saskatchewan and Manitoba as well. It is relatively easy to draw up your own will as long as you have a guide to assist you. If you have a complex situation, such as trust arrangements and a substantial estate, you should see a lawyer. His or her charges for estate planning and drafting a will are in the area of $40 to $50 an hour but the money is well spent for the peace of mind it gives you.

The lawyer's function will be to draw up the document to carry out your wishes. He or she may suggest alternative ways of doing so legally and will advise you of any problems or possible causes of litigation in the plan you propose. It is not a lawyer's job to tell you how to distribute your assets, although you can usually discuss this and find out what others do. When you enter the office you should be prepared.

1. Have a list of all your assets, including loans against them and details of life insurance, private, industrial or government pensions.

2. Have a list of all debts.

3. Be prepared to state how you wish to have your estate divided. You may direct a final distribution of your property to certain persons and retain no further control over it. This may be all that you wish to do. If you want to maintain the capital intact and retain control of its disposition after the original beneficiaries have passed away, you may still do so by setting up a trust. This trust will set out your directions respecting the payment of interest earned to one or more beneficiaries during their lives and investment of the capital. It may also permit encroachment of the capital under certain circumstances and it may contain other provisions that you desire to include. The instructions then direct the final disposition after the original trust has been fulfilled. The use of a trust has different implications and you should ask for a comparison of the two methods.

4. If there are any special circumstances, such as a "common law" relationship, illegitimate or adopted children, separation or divorce, disclose them completely. Such situations may require special provisions to avoid litigation.

5. Know the things that are still unsettled in your mind and for which you wish advice.

6. It is usual to specify the investments which your executors may purchase if a trust is contemplated. You might indicate, if you so wish, what your executors should do with the assets and the form in which they should be turned over to the beneficiaries if a trust is not employed.

7. Be prepared to name an executor to be responsible for carrying out the terms of the will. If an individual, the executor should be someone capable of and willing to do this, and likely to survive you. Often this means a son or daughter. At one time it was frequently a friend or business associate but, in view of the work and liabilities involved, this is now infrequent. For the same reasons, the trust companies, who are professional administrators, are very generally employed. Their use is optional when the estate is simple and to be disposed of at once. However, when a trust (which may carry on for years) is set up, it would be prudent to provide for the services of a trustee who is most unlikely to die and will be there to carry the plan through to its completion.

8. If you own a property which is located in another province or country or securities of foreign origin, it would be wise to ask your lawyer if these are likely to cause any serious complications in settling your estate or will render it liable for additional taxes. In some cases, the jurisdiction in which the property is located or the security was issued, if different from your place of residence, will require clearance before releasing or transferring the item. This may entail substantial additional expenses. They may also claim tax upon it. If so, you might wish to dispose of it now and have the matter settled to your satisfaction.

Burial Plans -- The Unpopular Topic

It is generally agreed that it is a wise plan to make the decisions respecting your burial, hopefully long before the event occurs. To do so won't make any difference to you, but it certainly will to your survivors and, if you have made the arrangements, they will be spared the problem of doing so at a difficult time. To be realistic about this matter, there are very few of us who can face the job of going through the complete list of steps to the final one of arranging the details of, and perhaps preparing, the actual funeral. Under the stress which occurs at the time of death of a loved one, and the necessity of immediate decisions, often too much money is spent, and steps taken with which the deceased would not agree. Even those making the decisions are not sure of their desirability. The following is a partial list of things to be decided. Go as far as you wish but advise those who are likely to be responsible for their implementation what you wish to have done and of any actions you have taken.

It is probable that the most important thing is to ensure that any steps required to satisfy your own religious beliefs and those of your family are taken. Plans to ensure these will help with your own and your family's peace of mind. It is important to realize that your funeral should be conducted in a manner that will leave your family feeling satisfied that they fulfilled all of their obligations and desires properly.

The event will be a shock to your spouse, and any assistance you can render by making advance preparations will be a valuable and appreciated aid.

The first step is to decide if you wish cremation or burial. If the former, how will they dispose of your ashes? If the latter, where do you wish to be buried? Is there room in a family plot? If so, make this known. If not, the best time to find a plot is now, while you have the time to look around, make the selection, compare costs and then pay for it.

The final step is the actual arrangement with the funeral director. One hears constant complaints of the cost of funerals and constant replies from the funeral directors that the family asks for unnecessarily expensive caskets and trimmings. They suggest that this could be avoided by making suitable arrangements in advance. It is no doubt a wise step.

Acquaint the family with your wishes respecting the actual service, but let them have one which will, in particular, satisfy your spouse so that he or she will feel that the last act for you was in keeping with his or her beliefs and wishes.

Finally, should you wish to become better educated on this whole subject, consult "Death & Dying In Canada," another in the Self-Counsel Series which gives you many facts and hints on the do's and don'ts in the funeral and burial business.

CHAPTER 13

THINK OF YOUR SPOUSE!

When making your will, changing life insurance or purchasing an annuity or pension plan, be sure to consider the position in which it will leave your spouse should he or she survive you. Often this is not thoroughly understood and bequests are made to children or charity without realizing that these may cause hardship to the surviving spouse. Therefore, you should take into account the changes which will occur in income after your passing and be certain to provide in full for your spouse first, unless you have made a decision to the contrary with full knowledge that you are doing so.

With the recent changes of death duties on property passing between spouses, it may be that there will be no taxes payable at that point. Your lawyer or accountant can advise you if anything will be payable in your case. For example, the province in which you dwell and the location of any assets may have a bearing on this, so each person's case should be considered on its merits.

If you wish to make bequests to others, you can do so by a trust with a life interest to your spouse as explained in the previous chapter. As an alternative, if you are content to do so, both partners can make their wills at the same time and word them to reflect their joint wishes so that the desired distribution will be achieved after each has passed away, regardless of which one goes first.

In either case, if desired, the surviving spouse has the assets or full income for life and bequests are left to others after this obligation has been fulfilled.

Changes in Income on the Passing of the First Partner

(a) Old Age Security Pension

This pension ceases with death. The living spouse, of course, continues to receive any pension already payable to him or her directly.

(b) Canada Pension

Providing a pensioner had contributed for one third of the number of calendar years possible, or for ten years, which is the smaller, or at least three years in any case, the surviving spouse of either a legal marriage or a common law relationship may be eligible for a monthly pension. So may dependent children. Enquire at the Canada Pension Plan office if you think you may be eligible.

There is a death benefit which is a lump sum of basically six times the monthly pension. If the contributor had never received a pension but was contributing to the plan, on death it is assumed that he or she had reached sixty-five and a pension is calculated on which to base the survivor's benefits. In either case, there is a monthly pension as shown below. The basis differs depending on whether the person has reached sixty-five. It also depends on whether or not he or she now receives a Canada Pension.

(i) If the survivor is under sixty-five, the pension (as of summer 1974) is $33.76 per month, plus 37-1/2% of the deceased's pension.

(ii) If the survivor has reached sixty-five and does not have a Canada Pension already, he or she receives 60% of the deceased's pension.

(iii) A surviving spouse already in receipt of a Canada Pension is entitled to the larger of either (i) 100% of the present pension plus 37-1/2% of the deceased's pension; or (ii) 60% of the present pension and 60% of the deceased's pension.

(c) Private or Industrial Pension Plans

Find out exactly what you are entitled to if you are enrolled in a pension plan. There are so many variations and it is very possible that, on the pensioner's death, there will be a basic reduction or complete cessation of the payments to the survivor.

(d) Other Benefits

Income from investments, etc. are probably unaffected but such things as bequests which have been paid to the deceased may be. Find out, if applicable.

(e) Your Life Insurance

So far, we have considered incomes which will be reduced by death. The major common source of a new flow of income is life insurance -- this was the original reason for its purchase. Earlier, the alternatives which could be selected instead of awaiting payment at death were considered. Some enabled you to retain the life insurance while using its cash surrender value to produce income and eliminate the cost of carrying it.

Your final decision respecting the dispostion of this insurance may now be determined more clearly after you have gone through this exercise of looking into the position of your spouse after your passing. You may direct, in your will, what is to be done with the proceeds, or simply make the policy payable to the beneficiary.

Keep in mind that the expenses at the time of death are quite substantial. There are the costs of the funeral, legal and probate, and executor's fees. There may be outstanding debts, and perhaps taxes, although these are unlikely on a small estate passing to a spouse. While costs will vary considerably with each case, it is unlikely that the couple who were used as our example in Chapter 5 (page 37) are likely to get by with expenses of less than $5,000 to pay funeral, legal and executor's costs when the husband passes, or the wife, if she has an estate to be probated. This means that half of the life insurance proceeds of $10,000 will be required to pay the expenses, with only the balance available for investment. When you make or review your will, you might ask your lawyer for an estimate of costs for handling your estate.

The first step is to read your policy to see what the company is legally obligated to provide or do for you. It no doubt pays the principal sum, less any loans against it, if you so desire. What would be the best use for this money? After the above-mentioned funeral costs and legal expenses, there may be a mortgage, debts, etc. which bear interest costs, and perhaps the best use of this money, or part of it, would be to pay them off.

For investment of the remainder, if any, there are Canada Savings Bonds and a great many fine types of secure investments available from such places as the banks and trust companies, which pay an historically high rate of interest. In addition, one may purchase a mortgage which yields a higher rate of interest still. There is also the full range of securities, stocks, bonds, etc. offered through investment dealers and brokers.

Your insurance policy may offer to pay an annuity and will provide optional plans. This is how it works. The policy pays its net face value on the death of the holder and in the policy provision is shown how much of different optional types of annuity can be purchased for each $1,000 of the proceeds. The size of the monthly annuity cheque which can be purchased with each $1,000 varies according to the type selected. For example, an annuity which pays for "10 years certain" means that, if the beneficiary dies in less than ten years, the payments will be made to some other designated person for the balance of the ten-year period. On average, this type of annuity will pay out more than one without this provision so it costs more and the purchaser will be able to buy less of it. This illustrates the necessity for careful consideration of these various types of annuity before making a decision.

The prices of each will be specified on it. However, they are probably out of date, as your policy was most likely written when interest rates were much lower. Your insurance company cannot give you less than stated on your policy, and, in fact, may offer you a much better annuity at the present time and as long as interest rates remain high. Ask if they will do so. You are at liberty to shop around to determine which company will give you the best annuity for your money and it is suggested that you do.

Your money may, also, be left on deposit with the insurance company to draw interest and the company will tell you what the current rate is. It varies from time to time, but will probably be much below the rate obtainable on investments which your executor or beneficiaries could purchase themselves later.

After deciding, therefore, on the most profitable way to handle your insurance policy, you will be able to make a reasonably accurate forecast of your spouse's income which will be somewhat as follows.

The figures given are for the situation in which the husband predeceases his wife and will not be the same if the wife dies first. If this occurs, a recalculation with the appropriate figures will be required.

In the preliminary estimate of retirement income made in Chapter 5, (page 37), two Old Age Security Pensions were included. Now one of these, $1440.72, will cease. The Canada Pension (assuming the widow is over sixty-five) will also be reduced by 40% or $576.29, a total drop of $2017.01 per year. How much will the widow's expenses drop?

The deceased's share of food, clothing, personal care, medical and health, cigarettes and alcohol and the life insurance payments will be eliminated.

This will total $1193.50 (page 45) and, if the wife gives up the automobile, this will cut costs another $744, thus increasing the saving to $1937.50 or $79.51 less than the reduction in income. Assuming that the husband had succeeded in making sufficient changes in his income to balance income and expenditures without having to earn wages which would now cease, his wife would be about as well off. However, the estimated income included earnings of $300 by the

wife. It may be that she is now at an age where it is not possible for her to continue with employment, and, if she stops
working, her money will have to come from either reduced
expenditures in other areas, or income from another source.

If there is no life insurance, the money for final expenses must be drawn from savings and investments which
will reduce her income accordingly.

With this information, it will be possible to write a
will, knowing what you actually have to dispose of and what
may be required to enable your spouse to live as you would
desire.

Explain It

Throughout this book, the desirability of the husband
and wife working together has been emphasized. Presumably, in the formation of the plans for wills, the discussions
have been joint and the final decisions mutually acceptable,
so that each partner's interests have been safeguarded. However, often the husband has looked after the major financial
affairs, with the wife perhaps handling household money.
Without further thought, he decides whether or not they will
make wills and what their content will be. The wife, in this
case, knows very little about what her position will be if the
husband predeceases her which, on the average, he surely
will. This is very common and, when it occurs, the wife is
faced with a multitude of unexpected questions which she
has not been prepared to answer. This is most unfair. The
husband knew the answers and could have quite simply in-
structed her. This would not have made her widowhood much
easier, but would have assured the consummation of your
wishes. So talk it over. She deserves it. Taking her into
your confidence and considering her desires will certainly
help your relationship. If there are things for which you have
not made proper provision, they may be revealed and provision made for them now.

Remarriage

Remarriage is something that should also be discussed long before one of the partners goes. This decision may be influenced by the terms of your will and its provisions may affect the surviving partner's happiness seriously. Try and think of the problem in terms of the survivor's position, and eliminate as much emotion and jealousy as humanly possible. The survivor will be left alone at a time when your children will have their own family affairs to concern them. There are few instances where the parents live successfully with their children and their families. Such relationships are usually not by choice, but necessity. Friends are also passing on and becoming more restricted in their activities. Single men and women are not often included in plans with couples. Loneliness is a very major problem. The support of a partner is needed more than ever. Remarriage at this stage seems to be most frequently contracted between old friends who already know each other well. Such a union brings additional financial strength because of the pooled income, companionship and the prospect of a few more happy years.

It frequently occurs that a widow or widower will hold back on remarriage stating, "I wish I knew what my late spouse would think about it." This could have been readily settled if the couple had told each other to remarry if desired. If it has not been discussed and an understanding reached, do it now.

Another point is that, if the will is left as a trust with income to the survivor, it frequently stipulates that income ceases on remarriage. Should you have a "dog in the manger" attitude and attempt to deny your spouse of this income through the provisions of your will? Do you really want to do that? Such a provision is probably often put in without proper consideration. If you and your partner worked together to build your estate, is the survivor not entitled to continuance of it if remarried? While your wife may not have held a paying job, your arrangement was that you brought in the money and she looked after the home and family. Can you in fairness cut off the pay for the job she did as agreed? Let your decision on this matter be one that is well thought out and mutually acceptable to both partners.

The Wife's Responsibilities to Her Husband on His Retirement

The problems a wife will have when her husband retires have been stated and a plea made for both an understanding of them by the husband and assistance to her in their resolutions. It works the other way around too. The retiring husband has been revealed as a man with problems. The gift of understanding assistance by the wife will make his transition much simpler. It is to her advantage to have him happy for two reasons. The first is that they are going to be together so much more, and no one wants a frustrated, grumbling companion. The second reason is that he is more delicate than he looks and may need her care if he is simply to survive as long as possible. She is the one who knows him best, can see any changes and should know how to handle him. Blanket directions set down here would fail to cover more than a very few situations because of the variety which will be encountered. The wife can use a combination of close knowledge of her husband, coupled with her woman's intuition to sense and solve them.

As seen earlier, the husband may have a very strong reaction to retirement unless preparation has been well made, and a sense of the futility of further living may set in. If it does, it may shorten his remaining life span. This is where you, his wife, come in.

The job gave him, in addition to the occupation of his time, a sense of importance and a pay cheque. Now he is important only to you and, instead of his bringing home that cheque which was the evidence of his value to the employer and the effort expended for you, the postman brings in several pieces of paper which he is cautioned not to fold, mutilate or spindle. He may think he did nothing to earn them. No one seems to need his advice, assistance or work. At least they don't ask for it, but many will want it if it is offered. The other problems which his retirement bring to you are of minor importance compared with this one. If your husband is sixty-five, he may, on the average, live seven years and you fourteen, depending on which statistics are used and how you interpret them. In that average there will be some who last only a few days and some who make a hundred. Your help may keep him with you for many more years. Often men, struck with the mental reaction mentioned above, seem to die in a relatively short time because of it or the diseases it may cause.

You are the one who can do the most about that hopeless attitude and change it into a zest for life. To start with, he should feel important and needed, and you are the one to whom he is important now. Make him feel it. Ask him to do things and indicate that you need that help. Make sure he understands that you don't know what you would do without his advice. Point out the successful accomplishments in his life and don't think there are none. Anyone who came through the last fifty years, and successfully raised a family, is to be congratulated. The pension cheques are coming in only because of that and, insofar as the Canada Pension is concerned, because he worked and paid for it! Make him understand that it was his past work which keeps these cheques coming today. If there are other sources of income which result from money saved, this is a major topic for satisfaction. There must be many things; seek them out and use them.

But this is of the past. It is in the future that you can perhaps do the most. The old man has had to do what the job or the boss scheduled for fifty years and he may need help and pushing to go out and get started in new activities on his own. You are the only one who can help him here. Listen, patiently; allow him to let off steam, encourage him to try and keep at it. He may be slow and hesitant, but you should persist gently. You must not fail.

This man is probably the most precious possession which you will ever have and he is virtually irreplaceable. So much of your time will be spent together. After those many years of marriage, there must be some very deep feelings. Nothing can be as remotely important to you as his welfare and presence. No doubt, like most men, he will have his small imperfections, but these are only annoying and of little importance compared with his loss. Don't nag him, let these small things pass unnoticed. Nagging only serves to drive home that sense of uselessness that he is fighting. Above all, if you are a perfectionist, don't expect him to be able to accept such values. Even a saint could not take this and to make his life miserable to achieve an end so empty is a short-sighted policy.

To help him work out a happy life so that he enjoys those retirement years will be the greatest contribution which you can make, not only to him, but to your own remaining time.

CHAPTER 14

WHERE WILL YOU LIVE?

HERE OR IN ANOTHER COUNTRY?

The changes introduced by retirement make it desirable to consider the suitability of your present home for building the pattern of your new life. There are three choices: remain where you are or, if you choose to move, relocate as close as possible to your present place, or move completely away from the area to a new environment.

Perhaps you have had a dream of moving on retirement to a location which would make a major difference to your happiness. There are many who do just that and write back to the folks at home describing the wonderful time they are having. But not all are so fortunate. Many return home disillusioned. Use caution, and be sure that the step is for you. If, after you have done the homework and your spouse agrees, go to it, and good luck!

The place which you establish as your residence may be the deciding factor on which the following are based. However, you must consider not only the Canadian law, but that of the country to which you move. Investigate regulations at both ends if you plan to go for more than a normal vacation.

If you cross the border and establish residence elsewhere, you may lose some of the government sponsored financial benefits. Know what this will mean to you and keep in mind that it may create tax complications. Here are some of the items which are often of sufficient importance to affect your decision.

The Old Age Security Pension

You will continue to receive this wherever you go if you have resided in Canada for a total of twenty-five years after reaching the age of twenty-one. Thus, many who would receive it in Canada would lose it on moving.

Canada Pension

Canada Pension is payable to the pensioner regardless of location of residence.

Capital Gains Tax

On moving to a foreign country, whether you sell your assets in Canada or not, a "deemed" liquidation has occurred in the eyes of the tax department, and any capital gain which would result, had liquidation actually taken place, becomes taxable. Thus, part of your income earning base may be lost if you emigrate. Find out.

Income Tax

If the assets from which your income will be derived remain in Canada, it would be desirable for you to check out what the tax liabilities will be. These may vary with the country to which you emigrate. Check there and here.

Health Insurance

Government supported health plans generally terminate. Some countries have plans of their own which may satisfy you. Others may not. Investigate this feature at any place you plan to take up residence. Some persons, who have disabilities which require costly drugs or treatment, or illnesses of which they can reasonably expect a recurrence, find the value of the protection provided by the provincial medical and hospital insurance which they may now enjoy is an asset which they cannot afford to give up, unless a similar one is available where they propose to reside.

The private plans available at the proposed new location may have unacceptable exceptions or may be too costly. The consideration is frequently the reason for deciding against moving.

Your provincial health plan may extend coverage that protects you when on a holiday outside your borders. If you plan to spend perhaps some months outside Canada, investigate the coverage provided during that period by any provincial health plan through which you have coverage.

Possible Language Difficulties

If you are thinking of moving to a country where a language you do not speak is spoken, consider the special difficulties. In many places, English or French is spoken but this may be confined to certain shops or a colony of visitors. Unless you are willing and able to learn the new language, the inability to communicate elsewhere may become irritating and this is frequently why persons who emigrate to, perhaps, Greece or Mexico eventually return home. The laws, too, are perhaps quite different, and you may not be happy while subject to them.

Where Should You Locate?

You may decide that you wish to move from your present home because it is no longer the best one for you in retirement. The possible alternative types of accommodation are discussed in Chapter 15 so only the factors affecting the selection of a suitable geographical location will be considered here.

Moving is an expensive and difficult step. It also means the loss of a familiar environment and old friends. A new location may bring new problems. Moving is a major step and it is unlikely that you will move unless there are compelling reasons for you to do so.

Retirement will require a new way of life, so to stay or not to stay is a question which must be faced. There are many important factors to consider. Weigh each one carefully and don't make a snap decision. Look at the changes which will occur in income, how you will spend your time and, especially now, maintain your health. Proximity of your family and old friends assumes a new and greater value.

It is probable that a husband and wife will view a move differently. The changes inherent in retirement are very different for each. The person retiring now has his or her whole day to re-plan and loses many things of value such as the companionship of a work group. The wife, if she has stayed at home, has her household routine as usual in the familiar setting. Her changes are a changed husband, the need to put up with his injection into her daily life and, perhaps, a reduced income. Moving away may be a greater adjustment for her than for him. She has made the home reflect her personality. It took time and money and has become part of her. Relocation means giving up something personally hers which she may not wish to do. The husband may welcome it as an opportunity to select a location because it will provide the recreation he has always wanted. It can be a very helpful thing for a man at this time and, indeed, he may have been looking forward to a move to some favoured spot as one of the main benefits of retirement. The old associations of the job with the home can be left behind and it will be easier to get into the new routine. A completely new list of interests will be introduced. To the wife it may be quite different. She must give up the familiar comfortable home and routine and start all over again to make a new dwelling into something which suits her and has all the "bugs" worked out of it. She may have to leave behind certain neighbourhood outside activities which may be an important part of her life. For these reasons, she may not view moving in the same light as her husband and considerable compromise may be necessary.

Therefore, approach the subject carefully and do not make up your minds without thorough consideration of all the factors. Take time to weigh them, for time often permits your mental processes to make a more objective evaluation and may assist you in deciding upon a mutually acceptable compromise. New ideas often frighten and one recoils from them but, with time, a more realistic picture forms. The good and bad points become apparent and a stronger and clearer decision comes into focus. It is one which can be more readily accepted and is more likely to be sound. The strength of emphasis which your partner places on each factor will come through, and it is essential that you understand this, as it will be one of the dominant factors in your own conclusion.

As you consider each factor, think of the points in favour of moving and those against it. There may be quite a long list on either side but, after all are weighed, some will soon become relatively unimportant. Others will gain dominance and one may soon emerge as the deciding factor which cannot be ignored. This will make your decision a definite one. Perhaps you will conclude that there is no other choice.

Financial Considerations

One of the first steps which was advised back in Chapter 5 was to consider your financial affairs and find out what your income will be when this retirement day has dawned. Presumably, you have updated the original estimates as you went along and the picture is now clear. If there is no financial problem, money will have no bearing on your decision to move. However, if there is going to be insufficient income to fulfill all desires, you should now be certain that you know what the shortage is.

If money is a problem, the time has come when you must act and a change in housing may be the answer. This is always a major step and you will have to consider first what type of accommodation will be satisfactory. Will it be a basic change from house to apartment or simply to a less expensive edition of what you now have? Size need not be the only factor determining the cost. The real estate advertisements at the time of writing reveal that approximately similar homes, in two different suburbs of the same city, vary by 40%. Each is connected by direct public transportation to the main centre -- the less expensive takes about twenty minutes longer.

The price differential might be the answer for you, particularly if you take a smaller place in the less expensive location. The reason everyone doesn't grasp this opportunity without further consideration is, of course, the fact that even this relatively small change in location can put a strain on visits to and from friends and family. In addition, it usually means a change in other locally-used facilities such as churches, clubs and shopping. These are all things to be considered.

If the financial change must be substantial, the contribution made by a change in housing can be increased either by accepting much less expensive accommodation in the same area or by making a move, if you live in a large city, to a small town or less expensive spot in the country. This can be a trying decision. Some feel that, if they must "come down" in living style, it would be preferable not to do so in the present locality. This might involve difficulty in the continued participation in previous activities and the maintenance of old friendships, so the advantages in remaining would be lost. The better solution might be to find a new location that brings fresh advantages from recreational or climatic standpoints, or a place for which you just have a personal liking. Often a move to a rural area brings additional savings of a major nature as well as those from housing.

If you have been a member of clubs in any major centre, the cost has undoubtedly become an important factor. Some persons are a member of more than one club, perhaps a golf as well as a general social and curling club. These expenses would certainly be considerations if you are under pressure to cut your spending. In a rural area, one can usually join golf, curling and any other clubs and participate in all the activities for a small fraction of the cost of doing so in the city. Clubs in a rural setting may not have as elaborate facilities as those in the city, but these may not be that important to you. The difference in cost, however, may mean simply that you can continue with the activity rather than being forced to discontinue it.

For those who are considering taking up golf or, perhaps, even curling for the first time, as a retirement activity, the cost of joining a club in a larger city might be prohibitive. Membership in a small town club could be much less. As an example, a large city club may charge the following.

Initiation	$2,000	
Annual Fees		$400
Annual Assessment		$100
Locker		$ 25
	$2,000	$525

Often there is a monthly minimum food and beverage bill which is charged whether or not it is used.

A smaller golf club, adjacent to a town and with a club-house offering some dining and snack bar facilities, might have the following charges.

Initiation	$250	
Annual Fees		$175
Annual Assessment		$ 25
Locker		$ 25
	$250	$200

There will probably be no minimum food or beverage charge.

Some smaller nine-hole courses where there is no club-house or locker room -- just a caddy shop -- will likely charge you only the amounts shown below and no other assessed costs.

Initiation	$ 25
Annual Fees	$100

In a smaller centre, too, transportation and parking costs are frequently much reduced. The cost of household services and repairs are often much lower. People are more likely to be accepted for what they are than what they have and the maintenance of a certain standard with its attendant expense pattern is not necessary. Adjustment to living on a lower income in a smaller centre is simpler and changes do not involve the same reaction from others which they may in the more rigid social strata of a larger centre.

Possibility of Employment

If we are considering financial problems, one of the important considerations in location is the possibility of employment, either full- or part-time. Post-retirement jobs are scarce so, if you want to have a suitable one, this will probably decide the location in which you will live. If this consideration is important to you, be certain of the job possibilities available in any place you plan to locate. In many "retirement communities," there are many job-seekers and very few opportunities. Some areas also refuse to grant work permits or licences to persons until they have resided there for a reasonably lengthy qualifying period. Check out all these things first to avoid serious disappointment.

A Location Which Brings Desired Activities

Your "business" home was probably located near the job and proximity to other interests was a secondary consideration in your choice. Now, the availability of the other interests can become the dominant factor in choosing a location. If you have definite interests which could contribute much towards a satisfying use of time, by all means do everything in your power to make it easy to pursue them. A satisfying use of time is of such major importance now that it is well worth making sacrifices in other directions, if necessary, to enable you to enjoy these activities.

Should You Stay Near Your Old Job?

Unless your previous employer is providing work for you after you have retired, you will likely find, as many others have, that the place where you worked has very little further interest in you. Your old friends there are now as fully occupied as you were. If you visit the plant or office, they are too busy to spend much time with you. It will be unusual if they need your advice and certainly the man who took your job won't want to admit that he can't do it without your help. All this means that it won't provide much of an interest, and to be near and not wanted by it may be disappointing. Thus, remaining is unlikely to be of value and may be a disadvantage.

Health

The maintenance of good health now is an important consideration. Moving to a new home, for all or part of the year, may be advised by your doctor. However, if you are not content in a new environment, you might do as much harm as good, so exercise considerable care in selecting a new spot. It is not unusual to meet many who moved to a more suitable climate only to find that the other disadvantages were too great and that they were not able to accept them or enjoy the new location. Soon they were back home again, sadder and poorer for the experience. If a move to another climate is desirable for health reasons, exercise care in selecting the spot. Take into account the factors discussed in this chapter.

Proximity to Family and Friends

Family and old friends usually mean much to retired persons, and one of the common reasons for coming back, given by those who moved away, is that they just missed them too much and nothing else took their place. Families cannot be replaced by new ones in another location and old friends take years to develop. Those who move into new locations report that, while newcomers are welcomed and included, no depth or real friendship seems to grow. One person moves out, another in, and no one seems to care. This type of association provides companionship but deep friendship takes longer to grow. Still, its development cannot be ruled out and companionship dispels loneliness and boredom if the companions are interesting.

Try It Out First!

If you do decide to move to some distant point with which you are not really familiar and the decision has been based on what others have told you or what you perhaps have seen on a short holiday in the region, this is not a good enough base on which to make such a serious decision. Too much of it reflects another person's opinion or the advertising which plays up the advantages. Even your own observations were made through the eyes of a tourist on holiday.

If you move there, you will be staying in a different place, doing different things and the attitude and glamour which comes with a holiday soon wear off. You indulged yourselves then and spent more freely than you normally do. You probably were there in the most enjoyable weather of the year. What will it be like when you must spend year after year there? Look at all aspects carefully. Can you afford it? Are there the activities you require, not only to use your time pleasantly but to provide those psychological satisfactions you require? Are there hospitals and medical facilities? What about that health insurance problem? Can you obtain the insurance you require? Is the climate, on a year-round basis, acceptable? If you have friends and family that mean much to you, will you be able to see them often enough?

There is only one way to answer these questions to your satisfaction, and that is to have a try-out before making a permanent move. You should actually live there for as long a period as possible before making the step a definite one. Rent the kind of living accommodation you plan to use. Move in as a permanent resident, not a tourist, and live as you plan to live. Try out the activities in which you plan to participate. Meet the people you will have to live with once you are there. Will you enjoy living with them? Stay on through the most unpleasant period of the year. Stay long enough for the novelty to wear off and the problems to develop. Rent out your present home for perhaps six months or a year. Any difference in cost will be well worth it, and will be much less than the cost of selling, relocating and then doing it all over again, if the move turns out to be undesirable.

The Retirement Community

A development of recent years which is catching on and growing is the "retirement community." Many of the early ones were not conceived as such, but just developed because they filled a need that was crying to be answered. The need existed for retired people who, when they found suitable spots, often in the warmer south, began to congregate with their trailers and mobile homes. This demonstrated that there was a need for properly planned communities, and some large, prosperous companies have grasped the opportunity to build towns which are specifically designed and located for retired people.

Are these good places to go? Perhaps not for everyone. It is easy to see that the accommodation in these places has been designed to take care of the specific needs of the older person. The apartments are equipped with such specialized conveniences as non-slippery floors and grab bars at the toilet and bath. Maintenance problems can be kept to a minimum and children's considerations have been eliminated. Schools are not required and recreation and medical facilities suitable for the older person have been emphasized. While these physical arrangements are desirable, the main advantage may be the availability of a large number of potential companions who have similar interests. Through them, loneliness can be avoided and the provision of a broad choice of activities specially suitable for the group is made possible. For the gregarious person who has decided to relocate anyway and who seeks and needs this type of life, it must have decided advantages. On the other hand, there are those who wish to live a quieter life and whose interests do not require the participation of others. They find the community too busy and their privacy often difficult to maintain. Once again, it's up to you to make the choice and fulfill your desires.

CHAPTER 15

YOUR RETIREMENT HOUSING

At each stage of your life, housing has a different function to perform. Its kind, size and location are determined by the necessities of the various levels of family life which follow in succession over the years. When the children are young, schooling and safety of access to it, availability of playmates and recreation areas and freedom from undesirable influences are very dominant factors. In addition, more space is required. Most of these factors have no value and are perhaps disadvantages after retirement. Any extra room, which is no longer used, is expensive to carry in terms of taxes, heat and upkeep. The money it is worth is tied up unproductively instead of producing income for you. Unless these costs can be offset by renting the extra space out, taking in boarders or "duplexing," you have sufficient reason to think about moving.

What should your living accommodation provide in retirement? Room for boisterous activities and insulation from neighbours which helped keep the peace in the family is no longer a need. A compact, easily-maintained area on one level, if possible, will reduce the physical demands. Low cost and upkeep will also be favourable factors. Access to good public transportation is usually desirable. Proximity to shopping areas and other facilities such as your church, a library and medical and hospital services is important. Try for a neighbourhood where other potentially compatible people of your age and liking are plentiful. Be close to any facilities you desire to make your use-of-time programme feasible. Remember, too, all those other reasons discussed in Chapter 14 to help you determine the geographical location in which your new home should be found. All these things are important. Decide which are "musts" for you and look for them in your new quarters.

Rental Apartments

The possible alternatives can be narrowed down if you have a financial situation which would favour rented rather than owned premises. Renting frees your capital for income production. An apartment with modern facilities and in a good location can generally be rented at a reasonable cost, largely because it is small and so many facilities are provided for joint use outside the living quarters. Small individual houses cost much more because of the less efficient use of land and utilities. As an example, one sees rental apartment buildings advertised for sale based on a value of $10,000 to $20,000 per suite. It would be impossible to buy a house of the same quality in a similar location at many times the price and you would not have such a wide choice in location, size and facilities offered.

The rental charged for such a suite will be much lower than the cost of carrying the comparable living space in the house, particularly if the house is mortgaged. This is because the taxes, interest and upkeep will be much smaller on the lower value of the apartment and many facilities will be available for common usage by all tenants.

Some rental buildings cater to young families, some to older persons without families. This can be important. (One person who lives in an apartment building occupied by her contemporaries reports that she can enjoy a card game every night with neighbours, without leaving the building! There is no physical effort required in caring for the lawn, building or snow removal. The cost is known, which is important to anyone on a tight budget and, if you wish to be free to travel or go off to the cottage, things will be looked after during your absence. For the retired person, there are a great many advantages to the rented apartment which were not important, and as often as not were drawbacks, when raising a growing family. These are the reasons why couples often move to apartments at or near the time of retirement.

Condominiums and Co-op Apartments

For those who want all the advantages of the apartment but do not wish to give up the possible advantages of ownership during a period of inflation, the rise of the co-operative apartment and the condominium has provided the solution. These apartments look like any others but, instead of being rented out by the owners, can be purchased outright. If you have money from the sale of a home, this solution will provide you not only with a place to live but also with an investment for at least part of the money.

Advantages of Owning An Apartment

Ownership has two possible advantages: first the fact that the property may rise in value if inflation continues, thereby providing a hedge against inflation. (It may also drop, if the market moves in that direction.) Secondly, it may reduce the impact of income taxes. This comes about as follows. Suppose an owner, after selling a house, has $50,000 left after expenses and invests the money at 8%. His income will be $4,000 and, if his tax bracket is 40%, his income tax will be $1,600. If, on the other hand, he invests the whole amount in an apartment, he will have no taxable cash income. This is a genuine saving and the cost of ownership will probably be lower than renting.

The owner of a building in which apartments are rented seeks a good return on his money and, in addition, probably has on the building a mortgage on which interest is paid. Rents must be high enough to pay not only the mortgage interest but also the interest on the owner's equity and, on top of this, provide a profit for the owner. Therefore, the owner of a condominium or co-operative should be earning a good tax-free return on his investment. To rent or to buy? It depends on how **you** feel about it. Some still prefer to rent.

It is usual for the retired person who sees a house and buys an apartment to come out with some surplus cash. In a multiple-occupancy building, the same amount of living area, as in a house should be cheaper but, at this time, one usually wants a smaller area. Buying an apartment may provide the best of all worlds -- for some a comfortable place to live, a continued stake in property ownership, plus the release of funds for investment. In this way, your home is paid for and there is new income in your hands for spending.

Owning a House

While renting an apartment may bring relief from the responsibilities of ownership for many, there are others, particularly men, who cannot be happy with that solution. First there are those who have enjoyed doing the repairs, redecoration and renovations and who may enjoyably, and perhaps profitably, spend some of the new leisure time available in doing work of this nature. Secondly, there are the fellows or their wives who enjoy gardening. Their extra time in retirement will enable them to pursue their hobby more fully, to start plants indoors under lights, to transplant at exactly the right time and to see that all care is given when needed. It is surprising how far some go with this interest once the time is available, and pleasant to see the depth of satisfaction which can be derived from it.

Neither of the types above can live as happily in an apartment as in a house. One hears of many who try but who miss their interests so much that they are not happy. If you are likely to be one of these, think very carefully before taking an apartment. If finances and cost are the problems, consider a house in a less expensive area. If you search, you will probably find a compromise that will provide you with the means to enjoy the interests that a house makes possible, as long as you are willing to give up some of the less important things which you may not really miss. For many, it is also important to have the feeling of security and belonging that comes with ownership and the putting-down of permanent roots. They feel that they are still part of the familiar and continuing scene. Some who sell a house and rent an apartment may feel that this act removes them from that familiar setting and places them in a strange and insecure environment. So, even if buying a house does cost more, it just means that you pay for your hobby by spending more to have the home you want. The other fellow may spend the same amount in club memberships to pursue his interests. As usual, you make your own choice. If you have decided you like your present location and the size of your home and operating costs are the only problems, duplexing or renting rooms, as discussed elsewhere, may provide a satisfactory solution.

Mobile Homes

Just what is a mobile home? If you have not been in a modern mobile home, you may be very agreeably surprised when you see through one. The increase in the sale of mobile homes for use as permanent dwellings has been rapid. Industry figures quote sales of 3,075 units in 1963 increasing to 25,029 units in 1972. The second figure would comprise 17.8% of the total of all single detached houses sold in Canada that year. This is up from 3.8% in 1963, which indicates a very marked change in public acceptance of this type of housing. If you visit dealerships where these are sold, it will soon become apparent that retired couples are buying many of them.

There are two types of mobile units which are frequently confused. The "trailer," that house on wheels which is towed behind an automobile provides temporary, compact accommodation that can be taken along as you travel. While it is very suitable for this purpose, most would consider it too small and cramped for a permanent residence, although some are so used.

The "mobile home" has a somewhat similar exterior appearance to a trailer but is much larger. In spite of the name, it is no longer really mobile in the same sense as the trailer. It is, usually, much too large to be towed by an ordinary automobile and no longer is equipped with its own wheels. It is taken on a large truck to a location where it is set up on a permanent foundation. (It is now common to build a basement and place this "mobile" on top.) In reality, mobile homes are factory-built homes, designed so they can be transported as units then set up on permanent foundations and left there the same as any other house.

Regular "parks" provide sewerage, water and electricity which are permanently connected. The unit is mobile when compared with a standard house only in that it can be easily picked up from the foundation and moved to a new location if and when desired.

The purpose of these units is to provide permanent dwellings. They are well-designed, durable and many are built by old, established, reputable companies. They come in either single or double widths. The singles are about eleven to fourteen feet wide and frequently as long as sixty-five feet. The doubles are now becoming common. These are built in two sections, divided down the middle so that the two halves, when assembled side by side, make up dwellings which are approximately twice as wide as the single units. They must be built in this manner so that they can be transported by road in the usual way and joined together on the site. They provide homes of more common proportions up to twenty-eight feet in width, which permits wider rooms and a centre hall. They are spacious and may have in each a living room (16 feet by 13 feet), a dining room, den, one to three bedrooms, kitchen, utility room and bathroom. While there is the usual variation in price, in most, the bathroom has modern coloured fixtures, built-in vanity and counter-top. It is complete with mirrors and exhaust fans. Size and space is little problem unless one is looking for unusually large rooms.

The mechanical appointments and appliances are modern and smart. The kitchen usually rates praise from the ladies! Equipment may include modern freezer, refrigerator, electric or propane stove, double stainless steel sink, and built-in cupboards and counters. Each model is usually offered in an assortment of interior decorator designed colour schemes. Some even have wood burning fireplaces. It is fair to state that these are not makeshift contraptions, but proper homes.

Acceptance of new ideas in the home field is always slow, and such was probably true in this case. However, now recognition has arrived. Frequently financing was not easy and often was restricted to automotive terms and rates. Now some units, provided they are located in approved sites, are CMHC (Central Mortgage and Housing Corporation) approved and regular long-term mortgages are available from the usual lenders. Prices of suitable units as described above were quoted from approximately $11,000 for a one-bedroom model to $25,000 or more for the larger deluxe models (March, 1974). Used ones are usually available for less. Most prices included appliances, taxes, delivery and set-up charges within a reasonable distance.

When one purchases a standard house, the lot is part of the package. But, in the case of mobiles, the job is only half done; the location on which to place it is usually an entirely separate deal. This is not always true, as some parks do provide the site and home.

One should not, of course, purchase the home until the site has been selected and obtained, possibly the most difficult part. One is not free to park the unit on any available land that can be purchased or rented. There are no nation-wide universal rules. Most regulatory by-laws are made by, and are under the control of, the province and the local municipality. There is little uniformity. In some rural areas, there are practically no restrictions, and one sees these homes located all through the country in such districts. In others, they are treated the same as a conventional structure and must conform to the land-use by-laws.

In other places, municipalities have permitted separate sites to be set aside and used for mobile homes with specific provisions for them. These parks provide water, sewerage, electricity, paved streets and other services. Some are on the outskirts of towns and all their amenities may be used. Others are set up as independent communities with facilities of their own. The trend appears to be along this line, with large, well-financed companies entering the field. The development may cover hundreds of acres and provide room for hundreds and even thousands of homes. The location may have recreational facilities and a shopping centre as an integral part of the community. Some cater to all comers, but others restrict themselves to retired persons. In these parks, the lots are rented by the month and the rent usually includes water and sewage services. From there on, there is no iron-clad policy. Rents vary with the location and the quality and quantity of services offered. Obviously, the cost of renting a lot in an undeveloped rural setting is going to be small, and it is possible that an inexpensive water supply will be available and satisfactory provision for sanitary facilities can be installed privately.

At the other end of the scale is the lot which is on high-priced land skirting a metropolis and on which paved roads, a sewerage system, water and electricity supply have been installed. It may also provide a community centre, recreational facilities, etc. which are included in the rent. You get what you pay for. If you are interested, investigate the cost in the location which appeals to you.

One thing does seem apparent, that it is possible to sell an unmortgaged regular house for enough to buy a good mobile home and still have enough money left over for investment which could provide the income to pay the land rent and operating costs of the mobile home. This means that the move would save the operating costs of your present home and the extra money would then be available for other purposes.

The advantages would appear to be that the mobile is readily available at a firm price, in a finished form, often for immediate delivery. The most suitable home and lot can be selected separately and combined. The home can be purchased, and often financed, if you wish, and the lot can be rented, a choice not usually available in a regular house. The cost of the mobile is usually less than a house. It is frequently possible to select a retirement group for its location, if you so desire, but the home can be moved to another location at will.

There are, however, disadvantages, some of which may be as follows. There are no lots available in the central areas of most cities and location is restricted to more rural settings. Many, however, do have direct connections by public transportation to towns and cities. The municipal by-laws tend to be more restrictive than with regular housing. The lots in the park are usually not for sale which eliminates the possibility of ownership of the land for those who so desire. In some areas, resale prices are low, so check and see if this applies in your locality. If so, perhaps this can be to your advantage in that you might purchase a used unit at a considerable saving.

A Residence With Medical and Nursing Services Available

Nothing generates as many heated and obstinate statements from retired persons as the mention of going into a "nursing home." It is unfortunate that this is so and, for a starting point, let us realize that the first thing wrong is the inaccurate use of the term "nursing home." This designation is erroneously used to describe everything in the field from a luxurious private apartment hotel building in which medical and nursing care and food services are available if desired, to a home where persons completely incapable of looking after even minor functions for themselves are fully cared for. To some, it also includes the old-fashioned "poor house" of Charles Dickens' days. Most discussions on this topic are, therefore, conducted in a heavy fog of ignorance and misunderstanding. They always seem to carry a derogatory connotation and infer the idea of charity. Perhaps the loss of personal freedom is feared. Charitable homes may be available to those who require them, but those which we are discussing here are privately owned businesses, operated to make the owners a profit. They must please their customers or go out of business!

It is too bad that such an attitude generates so much feeling because it prevents proper consideration and understanding of the facilities available. There is a great need for retirement homes and those who are considering them should not be discouraged from doing so. The growth of these homes has been rapid both in number and, through knowledge and experience of the requirements of their customers, in quality.

One of the most useful things which could be done in this area would be to clarify and properly classify and name each type so that those interested could identify the kind under discussion. This would separate the groups, which is desirable as there is little similarity between them.

Let us make it clear at this point that the specialists in the field do agree that it is best for older people to operate on their own if possible. There is no move afoot to round up all older persons and to segregate them in some sort of an institution. It is recognized that they will retain their abilities better and longer if they use them on their own behalf, and any special provisions should be made only for those who require it. The Victorian Order of Nurses, or some service, may provide all that is needed in most cases.

What living accommodation then, is available that goes one step further than the regular apartment house, and what extras are provided? The variety is wide and the governmental, social and private operators are attempting to identify and fill all needs. The first type is, perhaps, one step removed from the regular apartments. Tenants often have one large room per person or couple with a private

bathroom, good cupboard space, etc. They may use some of
their own furniture, pictures and ornaments, which enables
them to bring a few of the familiar mementos of their lives
with them. There may be a common room with television and
a dining-room where meals are served. Breakfast may be
delivered to each room. Often there is a resident nurse and
a doctor on call.

Just what is the difference, then, and what are the advantages? Understand clearly that anyone can come and go
without any constraint just as one would in a regular apartment. Meals are provided, eliminating shopping and preparation. Nursing and medical services are available and
often included in the price. This may be an important comfort. Loneliness is often one of the difficult problems of older
persons, and here one lives with a group which can provide
instant companionship. What better place to find, perhaps, a
real friend? There are usually activities such as bingo, cards
and dances. Such a residence has been a most happy home
for many who have no handicap and don't need the extra facilities but who simply enjoy living in this atmosphere. Others
with some physical or medical disability find the provision
for health care a very helpful form of security.

Most of these organizations are providing very comfortable lives for their tenants. Still, many uninformed persons continue to think of them as very different places from
what they are. Perhaps it would help if they were called
"retirement apartments," or some similar name which removed them from the "old persons' home" category and
brought them back into the regular world. They are not the
answer for everyone. The person who must have his garden,
a basement workshop and who makes his own opportunities
may find that these are essential to his happiness. The
"loner," who just can't stand crowds and does not enjoy
group activities does not fit in here. Too often those responsible for the welfare of older relatives know of one person
who is happy in such a residence and, without stopping to
compare the two persons, accepts this as the answer for the
second. It may not be so, for their relative may have a personality unsuited for this life.

Beyond the apartment and hotel described above, one
may go through a progression of places ranging from those

where only slightly more care is given, up to those where patients receive what is equivalent to full invalid's bed care.

Should you consider some such place for your home? Once again, it depends on you. If you are still active, but enjoy group companionship and activities and would like to give up meal preparation, this may be for you. Many are happy in these circumstances. If you have some disability, it may be a very desirable and comforting move. If you have a health problem, there may be very little alternative. Proper care may be essential. This is a matter to discuss and decide with your physician. It is a step which becomes desirable with increasing age and essential if a disability develops. Often the older person will not give in, stubbornly insisting on remaining independent, past the time when it is really possible. The attempt to carry on alone is conducted under great difficulty and strain, and peace of mind or happiness is not possible. Friends and relatives are greatly distressed. Don't fool yourself, face facts. Such a person is much better off in a place where the care and comfort to which he or she is entitled is provided.

CHAPTER 16

SHOULD YOU CHOOSE EARLY RETIREMENT?

As a general principle, most persons who have worked all their lives are wise to continue working as long as they are physically and mentally able to do their jobs without undue strain, are reasonably happy to do so and are permitted by their employer to continue. The main exception would be those who have some alternative available which they understand and can afford, and at which they would be happier than at their present work. Retirement without these factors may bring problems as we have seen, and their solution has been the topic of this book.

Early retirement increases the magnitude of the basic problems which concern the retired, in particular money and the use of time. If one plans to live on pension, retirement before the sixty-fifth birthday may not be feasible unless you have personally made adequate financial provision for it.

The Old Age Security and Canada Pensions cannot start before that age. Private and industrial pensions are normally geared to commence at sixty-five but can usually be started at an earlier date if required. Each one differs, according to its terms, but to start it at sixty instead of sixty-five may mean as much as a 50% reduction in the monthly cheque. If you are considering early retirement and have such a pension, find out the extent of the reduction if the starting date is advanced. Most tax and other benefits cannot start until the sixty-fifth birthday has been attained.

All this is not to say that early retirement is not possible for financial reasons. It is simply to alert you to the problems. However, signs are everywhere that this situation will change just as many others have done in the past few years. The retirement age continues to come down and the government concern for the retired increases.

If you decide on early retirement, there are ways of handling the matter. First, your retirement savings plan could be designed with this in mind. If, for example, you plan well in advance to retire at sixty, you might simply start five separate registered retirement savings plans (there is no limit on how many you have) so that one can be cashed each year to provide the necessary income. This would fill the gap until the other pensions start at age sixty-five.

The second problem, the use of time, will mean that you are leaving your regular employment at an age when you are younger and may desire more activity than you will when you are older. It does, however, make you available for re-cycling into another more desirable job, or part-time work, at an age when you are likely to continue for a number of years.

There is considerable discussion about early retire-ment, normally from three separate groups. The first is, of course, those who have some very definite interest which they wish to pursue. It may be part-time employment or the ownership of a small business, both in fields which attract them, or it may be a complete cessation of work to partici-pate in a style of life which they feel would be highly desir-able. The second group consists of the young people who often talk blithely about early retirement and make statements, that are not generally well thought out, about how they plan to retire early and enjoy life. At that age, anything looks possible in the future. If you ask the speakers what their plans are for saving for that retirement, the answer usually is that they have none. Their plans for the use of time are generally rosy pictures of their last vacations which they imagine can continue indefinitely after retirement. If they do want to have an early retirement, well and good, but they should prepare financially and mentally for it and now, when still young, is the time of life to start doing so. As pointed out in Chapter 17, regular savings add up very rapidly over the years and make possible the attainment of very substan-tial goals. If ownership or part-ownership of a small business is desired, work towards it. This is a very reasonable and worthwhile goal. There is time to plan, initiate and bring to fruition those post-retirement aims.

The third group includes those who hold responsible positions and who are in their late fifties and early sixties.

Their strength is waning, the job demands are not, and the young men are breathing down their necks awaiting their departure. They cannot ease off and the strain is becoming too great. They would sincerely like to retire early but either financial needs or the question of what they would do with their time prevents them from doing so. If things are this difficult, surely a much better life after retirement can be planned even if it does mean some decrease in income.

Those in the above position should reconsider their financial picture and the possible ways of working it out to finance retirement. Look into the suggestions made earlier in Chapter 7. They apply equally well to the person retiring at any age. At least, do not lose by default. Consider the matter thoroughly and make an intelligent decision. More people every year are accepting early retirement as the solution.

Should You Then Retire Early?

The answer as usual to any question related to retirement will be a personal one. You know the present situation with respect to your job, health, income and state of happiness. How is your spouse finding life with you?

Balance this against the alternatives. If you retire, how will you be situated financially? You know how to calculate this, and don't act until you have done so. What will you do with your time? Do you have feasible plans for its use? How essential is a change for your health? Be realistic, think it through clearly, and be sure your spouse understands it. When both pictures are in focus before you, it should not be too difficult to decide.

CHAPTER 17

PREPARATION FOR RETIREMENT

One does not spend much time in discussion with retired people without being told that they wish that they had begun to prepare for retirement much earlier. It is an issue easy to forget when it seems so far away, yet it is so important and final when it arrives. If you are one of the lucky ones, believe it or not, it will also arrive for you. At that time, some advance preparations may make it so much easier and enjoyable.

By the time you have read this far, it must be clear that there are two major areas in which any retired person must come to a satisfactory solution. The first is financial, because how much discretionary income you have available to spend as you wish is going to determine what you can afford to do with the second, your use of time.

The Use of Time

This has been discussed fully in Chapter 8 (page 67) and need not be considered further here. Remember, however, that the further ahead one plans the better one will be prepared to use that time when retirement comes.

Financial Preparations

Obviously, the longer the period you have to prepare your finances the greater the change which you can make. The accumulation of money, or income, which is what you are saving it for, will increase with time, the rate at which you add to it and the rate at which its earnings are compounded. At any starting point, you cannot revert and start earlier, so that is fixed. The rate of saving has a high degree of flexibility, for it is simply the decision to defer spending from the present to the future. It is not easy; there are many demands on you every day. There is the desire to keep up with your friends who seem to have more and who like to live it up, put on the dog or, preferably, the mink and make it look as if they are better off than you are. Most of us are too competitive to accept that without trying to equal it. We enjoy indulging our families, perhaps more than is good for them.

Remember the earlier statement -- after sixty-five the old lady needs cash? The old man does too. It may mean continuing to play golf because he can afford to rent an electric cart to keep the exertion down to his limits. Twenty years ago he could walk.

It is never too late to start organizing your financial affairs well and even a very few years of effort prior to retirement may make a substantial difference to your income. Often the heaviest expenses occur just before the children leave on their own and then suddenly cease at an age when there are still sufficient years to enable you to weigh in with a substantial accumulation. At the same time, your income is reaching its peak and your mortgages are paid off. Savings will add up rapidly.

If you have been successful in keeping a programme going over the years, it snowballs as interest compounds on the interest and the totals start to surprise you! Ask retired people if, in their opinion, this would be a worthwhile idea to follow!

The Registered Retirement Savings Plans

The introduction of the registered retirement savings plan concept has opened new avenues for saving for those eligible to use them. Information is available from any bank or trust company and also other sources. There are many different plans. Some have guaranteed values, others fluctuate with the value of the investments made for them. All usually specify how the savings will be invested. Other plans offered by certain trust companies permit you to select the investments and the company carries out your buy-sell instructions. You may also put presently-owned investments into the plan provided they meet the requirements. The trust company charges a small fee for administering the plan.

At the time of writing there are guaranteed plans available offering a compound rate of around 10%. This is, of course, subject to revision as interest rates fluctuate. The examples shown below are calculated at a more conservative 8% as 10% may not always be available.

Within the prescribed regulations, the amounts put into the plans are income tax exempt. Before the introduction of this rule, a substantial part of your income might have been taken in taxes and would not have been available for spending or saving. Using the registered retirement savings plan as the method makes larger savings much easier. The savings in the plan can be withdrawn at any time, but it should be understood that, if the accumulated capital is withdrawn as a lump sum, this sum is added to your taxable income in the year of withdrawal. This is not so if it is used to purchase an income-averaging annuity. Your savings are, therefore, not locked in until retirement. You can, also, have a number of small plans instead of one large one to facilitate a withdrawal of part of the total. This would enable you to cash just what you wished each year, and would avoid the payment of tax on income you do not require and the drawing of all savings in one year which may perhaps put you in a higher tax bracket.

One of the advantages of the plan is that contributions may be deducted during periods of high earnings and income tax and may be withdrawn after retirement at, perhaps, a time of lower income and taxation. In the meantime, you continue to earn interest on the tax savings. Consider the possible advantages of saving $1 per year and depositing it in a retirement savings plan which could, at 8% compound interest, build up $185 (less the nominal handling charge) at the end of thirty-five years. That's right, $35 grows to $185 in that time. Larger deposits would result in proportionately larger accumulations. What would this do for you? The money in the plan can only come out in either of two ways, the first being to buy an annuity. Here, at present rates, your $185 would buy something just under $18 per year for life at age sixty-five. So, $1 per year from thirty to sixty-five means $18 per year for life after that. The second option is to draw the $185, pay income tax on it and invest the balance. If your rate was 40%, you would retain $111. Investment at 10% would mean $11.10 per year, and the $111 cash would remain for your heirs or estate after you have passed on. Would you miss $1, $100, $1,000 or more per year now, particularly if you can see these retirement benefits later?

Accumulation of Contributions and Compound Interest in a Registered Retirement Savings Plan at 8% Per Annum Net After Management Fee (often 1/4 of 1%)

Amount Per Year Invested	Number of Years	Total Accumulation
$1	35	$ 185.72
$100	35	$ 18,572.00
$1,000	35	$185,720.00

If you were able to start only in a small way but increase your contribution at ten-year intervals, a possible result would be as follows.

Contribution	Interval
$ 100	1st to 10th year
$ 500	11th to 20th year
$1,000	21st to 30th year
$2,000	31st to 35th year

Total accumulation at the end of the period would be $71,177.

If you started at age forty and saved $1,000 per year, invested as above, by age sixty you would have a total of over $49,000. These figures illustrate the power of regular saving and compound interest. You are free to set your own programme.

A Private or Employment Related Pension

Unless you start early in life, a private pension plan is very expensive. Today, the registered retirement savings plan is a much better method of preparing for a pension. Where possible, you should consider using it.

However, you may have employment where a pension plan is a "fringe benefit," and, if so, don't underestimate its value. Some plans require no contribution on your part, the employer contributes it all. In many, both contribute. If your employer has a plan, it is probably mandatory to participate. Once in, don't lose your benefits without considering the matter. With increasing inflation, the benefits of some plans have been raised voluntarily by the employer. And it can happen again.

Keep in mind what a pension may mean to you at retirement time. Until recently, such pensions were not common and the cost prevented many businesses from adopting a plan. Now they are becoming and will become more common. Most employees did not appreciate the value of a pension and often lost their pension rights by changing jobs without even considering the value lost. They often "bought out" their rights for an unimportant cash sum which was spent currently. After all, who planned to retire? Portability, the right to take your accumulated pension rights with you, was rarely built into these plans. Now there is a law dealing with and affording some protection in this regard. Anyone is wise to find out what pension rights may be lost if he is considering a change in employment.

Develop Your Interests

(a) Hobbies

It also becomes evident that those persons who enjoy themselves are those who develop many personal interests of a kind that can be continued after retirement. Often these are carried on in a minor way during their working lives, but are of real interest. Retirement is awaited eagerly for it provides the opportunity to exploit the interests more fully.

Hobbies frequently are learned by taking lessons and accumulating any necessary equipment so that, by the time retirement arrives, there is a genuine, well-founded activity in progress at a satisfying level.

Plan Ahead for Employment

It is important to plan head for work, either of a volunteer or paying nature, if that is what you wish, particularly if it is to be at a senior level. If you are employed in a responsible job requiring the energy of a young person, and the company policy indicates retirement from it at the regular or perhaps an earlier age, it is wise to look ahead and to switch some years in advance to an alternative job that will permit continued employment to a more advanced age. If there is no such possibility in your company, you may wish to look elsewhere. Remember, it is much easier to get the desired job while you are still employed than after you have retired.

Volunteer Work

In volunteer work, age will perhaps not be a bar to continued participation. If you wish to have a responsible position, it will probably mean putting in some years of work at the lower levels with progression upward as those ahead give up their jobs. If you plan well, you will be moving into the senior levels at the desired time. Without the years of earlier participation, it might be more difficult to get these positions when you want them.

Look For Your Retirement Home

If you look forward to retirement, you will be thinking well in advance about your home and the best location for it. You may holiday in different areas and make a careful selection over the years. If you make a selection prior to retirement, the new home may be ready when the event takes place.

Starting this preparation in advance requires first a plan and then continued effort to carry it out. Revise it as you see fit. Choose an investment and saving programme, get started, contribute what you can from year to year. Don't be afraid to start in a small way. By all means participate in the activities suitable for younger and middle-aged persons during these periods, but be prepared to grow into those more suitable for the later years when they arrive. Remember to develop interests jointly with your spouse. This relationship between the two of you will have a much greater importance once the demands of children and job have gone.

There is no set point at which one should start preparations; the earlier the better. However, this need not discourage those facing retirement shortly or, for that matter, those who already have reached it. If retirement is coming soon, start at once to get your affairs in order. Make those changes discussed in "How to Increase Your Retirement Income" in Chapter 7, and start to adjust your thinking to your life in retirement. Then begin to live that life in advance and work into it slowly. One of the best approaches is, during the last two years of your working life, to adjust your spending to live on the income you expect to have after retirement.

This will help you to understand that changes, if any, are going to be necessary. You can make desirable adjustments and go through the experience in steps. As a gradual process there will be less shock and you will still have the support of your job. Channel as much of your time into retirement activities as possible and build up a reserve of things you want to do but which must await more time. Remember, back near the beginning of this book, it was indicated that, on the first morning of your retirement, "all is silence and nothing will happen unless you make it do so?" Your preparation will eliminate these lonely, frustrating days. Instead, you can be awaiting the arrival of your retirement day to get at these things which you have in readiness.

The picture of that happy couple relaxing in the sun can be yours, but only if you make it come true. It's up to you!

CHAPTER 18

CONCLUSION

It would be unnatural to look forward to growing old, yet it is one of the inexorable laws of nature, and must be expected. It is escaped only by those who suffer the less desirable alternative!

Or is there an escape from growing old? One hears more frequently that, "you are only as old as you think," which implies that, at least mentally, one need not grow old. Perhaps there is something to this. While physical deterioration may come, as long as one's mental powers remain active, it is possible to lead a very satisfying and useful life. Your activities may be different from those of younger years, but so are your needs and goals. Change is not new with retirement, but has occurred with every stage since birth.

Success will be a matter of attitude and your degree of achievement in adapting to retirement. If one is satisfied and mentally fulfilled, what more can one ask? How often we see these older persons enjoying life and looking forward to the days ahead. They still think of themselves as young and continue to plan and look forward, quite satisfied with their lives. There was little more to be expected from pre-retirement years.

The purpose of this book has been to enable you to understand and know of the opportunities and pleasures available in retirement, to assist in the formation of your life and to help you adapt to it.

If it has wahsed away the fears, and engendered an attitude that sees this time before you as a pleasant, useful opportunity, then its success has been achieved.

No previous generation has been given an opportunity approaching yours. The building materials are all there, now it is up to you to use them.

How fortunate you are to receive so much! There is this land, so generously endowed. Be grateful for those many generations who have gone before to prepare it for you. Remember those who discovered its shores, travelled its breadth, defined its boundaries and showed the way for others to follow. They came, cleared the forest, tilled the soil, built their homes and founded the nation. Their successors have continued building to this day and have forged a home-land unequalled in this world. Many of those generations answered the call to keep it free. They gave their lives, their health and their best years to do so.

What these people have built they left behind for the coming generations to use and enjoy and now it is your turn to do so. Use and enjoy it well, or all has been in vain. As others have made this possible for you, now you are obliged to preserve and increase this heritage and to pass it on to the succeeding generations. To the extent that you have nurtured and increased it, you may be proud.

Then let one of the goals of your years be to use it well to achieve your own happiness and to contribute towards the making of a better world for those who share it with you now, and those who will follow afterwards.

CHECK LIST FOR RETIRING

At Once

1. Obtain all details respecting pensions and insurances -- group, life, income maintenance, health and disability insurance policies offered through group plans at your place of employment. Know the benefits you are entitled to while employed there and the options open to you on leaving or retiring.

2. Examine details of personally owned life insurance, pension plans or registered retirement savings programmes. Consider changes as suggested in Chapter 7. Do not delay finding these facts until retirement. They should be part of planning all your personal programme.

3. Obtain birth or baptismal certificate.

One Year Prior to Retirement

4. Discuss with employer his policy respecting retirement, options for continued employment and all benefits and options you may have.

Six Months Prior to Sixty-Fifth Birthday

5. Apply for Old Age Security Pension.

On Retirement

6. Meet with responsible officer at place of employment. Discuss again all benefits to which you are entitled. Be sure to get wages, holiday pay and any cash coming from company benefit plans.

7. Apply at once for three weeks' retirement pay available from Unemployment Insurance Commission.

8. Obtain list of any health, medical and hospital plans which have been paid by employer but which you must now pay direct. Get instructions and forms and apply at once.

9. Obtain list of any options you have respecting group insurance, pensions, etc. Do not decide these in haste -- take information and decide carefully at home after receiving any advice you desire.

10. Apply for Canada Pension if sixty-five and eligible. If seventy years of age, apply for Canada Pension, if eligible, even if you continue to work.

11. Have medical and dental examinations.

12. Both you and your spouse make or review wills.